BELIEVING SCHOLARS

BELIEVING SCHOLARS

Ten Catholic Intellectuals

Edited by

JAMES L. HEFT, S.M.

Fordham University Press, New York, 2005

Library of Congress Cataloging-in-Publication Data

Believing scholars : ten Catholic intellectuals / edited by James L. Heft.—
1st ed.
     p.   cm.
   Includes bibliographical references and index.
   ISBN 0-8232-2525-9 (hardcover) — ISBN 0-8232-2526-7 (pbk.)
   1. Catholic Church—Doctrines.   I. Heft, James.
   BX1751.3.B45   2005
   230′.2—dc22   2005016812

Printed in the United States of America
07 06 05   5 4 3 2 1
First edition

Contents

Preface and Acknowledgments

JAMES L. HEFT, S.M.

I n any published work of this sort, many people have participated. I wish here to acknowledge several individuals who have made the Marianist Awards possible. First, thanks for the educational vision and administrative skills of Bro. Ray Fitz, S.M., the president of the University of Dayton for twenty-three years (1979–2002), and to his successor Dr. Daniel Curran, for continued support of this award. Thanks also to the Office of the Rector of the University, most recently directed by Fr. Eugene Contadino, S.M., for its contributions to various details of organization that made the visits of the Marianist awardees graceful occasions. And thanks to Ms. Carol Farrell, my assistant, who also helped with many of the details of the events surrounding these lectures, and the various receptions and dinners connected with them. Ms. Farrell also assisted me in the preparation of these lectures for publication. Thanks to Donald Wigal who prepared the excellent index for this volume.

I wish finally to express appreciation for Marianist educational traditions that bring together head and heart, theory and practice, leadership and service, and work to overcome many of the unfortunate dichotomies that characterize our lives and our institutions. Marianist brothers and priests live together as equals and collaborate with Marianist sisters and lay persons to create learning environments for Catholic education and leadership. I have been personally blessed to enjoy such an environment at the University of Dayton for over a quarter of a century.

FR. JAMES L. HEFT, S.M.
JANUARY 28TH, FEAST OF ST. THOMAS AQUINAS

Catholic Intellectuals: No Ivory Tower

JAMES L. HEFT, S.M.

N early a decade ago, the first volume of Marianist Award lectures appeared in print.[1] In the preface to that volume, I explained how the University of Dayton, founded by the Marianists (Society of Mary) in 1850, had been giving since 1950 an annual award to a leading Mariologist. Some years after the Second Vatican Council, during a period when many Marian practices fell into desuetude, so did the granting of this annual award. However, the commitment of the university to the support and continued development of its Marian Library remained firm. For example, the leaders of the university and of that library, especially Fr. Theodore Koehler, S.M., established in 1975 the International Marian Research Institute which, in conjunction with the Marianum in Rome, grants pontifical degrees in the field of Mariology.

In the mid-1980s the university decided to reinstitute the annual award, but with a slightly different focus: the award would be given to a Catholic intellectual who has made a major contribution to the intellectual life. Recipients were asked to speak about their faith and how it has influenced their scholarship, and how their scholarship has influenced their faith. Some of these Marianist Award lectures have been cited elsewhere, and sometimes even reprinted.[2] In this introduction, I will touch upon three themes that are critically important for understanding the situation of a Catholic tradition four decades after the Second Vatican Council and five years into the third millennium. The three themes that seem to have gained the greatest importance since the first volume of Marianist lectures was published are the following: (1) the Church as a community that both teaches and learns; (2) how people of faith fare in the academy; and (3) Catholic scholars and the "ivory tower."

THE CHURCH: BOTH LEARNING AND TEACHING

John Henry Newman was one of the first theologians to begin to spell out in detail the impact historical studies could have on our understanding of the Church and our faith. His studies of the early Church not only led him to leave the Church of England and enter the Roman Catholic Church, but they also led him to argue for consultation of the laity in matters of Church doctrine and for a clearer understanding of how, over time, doctrine itself might develop. Newman was made a cardinal in 1879, just when the then newly elected Pope Leo XIII was launching a revival of Thomism in the Church. Much of Newman's most creative intellectual work on, for example, the psychology of religious belief (*The Grammar of Assent*), cast its argument in empirical and developmental categories, and as a consequence left many Catholics at that time puzzled by—if not outright distrustful of—Newman's scholarship.

The bishops at the Second Vatican Council (1962–1965), called by some historians "Newman's Council," laid the foundation for a major shift in Catholic intellectual life when they called for less Thomism and a more biblically based and pastorally oriented theology for the Church. The bishops also called all Christians to a greater awareness of the sufferings and joys not just of fellow Christians, but of all of humanity. This heightened degree of openness rendered many Catholic thinkers more willing to learn from the "signs of the times" lessons that might not have been as clearly grasped apart from such openness. The bishops, then, called for a more historically and empirically enriched form of theological reflection in the Church.

The philosopher Charles Taylor provides in his lecture several examples of how the Church has learned from "secular" society. In one of his most striking examples, he explains how the Church would not have learned to carry through on certain of its fundamental insights had it not lost its privileged position ("Christendom") during the Enlightenment, and found itself, after the prodding of certain Enlightenment thinkers, some of whom were quite opposed to the Church, affirming in a fresh and profound way "human rights" for all peoples. On a more personal level, Cardinal Dulles admits in his lecture that while he could not accept idealism or materialism or atheism, he could nonetheless learn something from these systems of thought. Medievalist Marcia Colish makes it clear that Catholic colleges and universities will benefit greatly if they learn to sustain certain practices that form essential structures of the modern university—such as academic freedom and the courage to follow one's research wherever it leads. Journalist and religious writer Peter Steinfels makes his case that "liberal Catholicism," which keeps its ear to the ground for positive movements in the larger society, is what the Church teaches one hundred years later—that is, in Steinfels's judgment, it usually takes the Church about one hundred years to realize the truth of what liberal Catholics believed a century earlier. Finally, theologian David Tracy suggests that as the Church moves beyond some of the uniformity of modernity and begins to learn how to recognize and respect the "other" as other, the Church's own identity will become clearer even as we learn to accept an irreducible but not self-destructive pluralism among ourselves and within society.

That the Church teaches, and teaches authoritatively, has been understood and affirmed from the beginning. What is just as important, and what has been the object of study only more recently, is that the Church has to learn as well as teach. After all, Jesus in his humanity grew in age and grace and wisdom, as the Gospel of Luke reminds us (Luke 2:52). The Church also learns and even confesses its sinfulness, as Pope John Paul II reminded all Catholics to do as they prepared for the millennium. How the Church is to learn not only from its own members but also from others, and how the Church is to understand that even doctrine develops historically—these are major challenges that the addresses collected here help us to think more clearly about.

FAITH IN THE ACADEMY

The phrase "faith in the academy" admits of at least two quite different understandings. First, it might pose the question whether today we should have faith that the academy will achieve what it promises. Or it might refer to how religious faith—particularly, for our purposes here, Christian faith—fares in the academy, whether the academy is hostile to such faith, or whether such faith can benefit from some or all of the practices of the academy. Many books and articles have been published recently that explore both issues. I am most concerned here with the relationship of Christian faith and the scholarly life. I have already mentioned that Marcia Colish maintains a robust confidence in the potential of the academy which, if allowed to follow the norms of scholarly practice and life, will contribute to the life of the Church and the wider society. Cardinal Dulles's lecture includes his reflections on how his college studies, which did not include theology, at a secular university actually led him to faith and eventually to the Catholic Church. And it should not go unnoticed that a majority of the scholars featured in this volume are not at Catholic universities.

Conventional historical wisdom teaches us that the modern Western university is, in its broad outlines, a creation of the Enlightenment. None of these Marianist awardees indulge in "Enlightenment bashing," but several point out clearly some of the limitations of an epistemological tendency rooted in the Enlightenment: namely, reducing all reliable knowledge to only that which is empirically verifiable. Catholic scholars resist this reductionism. Again, theologian David Tracy roots all Christian theology in the most basic religious "forms" of the Bible; that is, prophetic utterances and meditative or wisdom observations. Predictability is an essential characteristic of modern science; prophecy, especially in the religious sense, is not a form of discourse characteristic of the academy. And while one may find in today's university a course on the Bible's wisdom literature, even the most renowned of faculty would hesitate to teach wisdom, either as a survey course or even more audaciously as autobiography. To be "objective" and to present as knowledge what can be "verified" remain dominant beliefs in today's academy, even though many thinkers have shown recently that even science is inescapably based on assumptions that cannot be verified.

Historian Jill Ker Conway reminds us that very accomplished nineteenth-century American women with graduate degrees—women who quite consciously set out to do good and ambitious things—still found it quite difficult to speak in their own voices. Agency, personal distinctiveness, the uniqueness of individuals and individual contexts, the now widely recognized fact that all conversations are rooted in communities of conversation, none of which is exactly the same—all these emphases on particularities have put strain on the Enlightenment's ideal that there is and should be one universally accessible rational form of discourse.

Few who are familiar with the history of higher education in the United States and Western Europe will be unaware of the dramatic changes brought about by the increasing number of women who after World War II sought a college education. And over the last twenty years or so, not only has the number of women equaled the number of men, but the fields into which women have entered have greatly diversified. Anthropologist Mary Douglas's autobiographical comments recount graciously how just after the war in England she entered an almost totally male world of higher education. Religious editor and writer Margaret O'Brien Steinfels describes in her remarks a "world historical shift" of women's lives and prospects. If Conway's nineteenth-century women scholars had trouble finding their public voice, the women of the late twentieth century have not, though the still largely male-led academy seems slow to integrate women with their scholarly ambitions, some of their special scholarly perspectives, and their family concerns—concerns that should have been uppermost in the minds of men from the beginning.

The fact that half of these lectures have been given by women scholars underscores the interplay between particularity and universality in gender. To be sure, these women address many issues, and gender is not the only context or scholarly topic of the lectures given by them. I wish only to suggest that the strains between particularity and universality would best be characterized not as polarizations or as dichotomies. Why? Because particularity and universality interact. Individuals come to understand themselves within communities, and specific events are best interpreted in their historical and political contexts. These larger frameworks of interpretation often manifest "family resemblances" if not the same universal truths. Legal scholar Mary Ann Glendon describes in her address how, in a process rife with conflicts and divergent forms of thought, people of very different backgrounds and different nationalities came together in the aftermath of World War II to come to some basic agreements on what constitutes human rights. Moreover, according to Glendon, the individuals who made the greatest contributions to articulating an international bill of human rights were Catholics who drew upon social teachings of the Catholic Church for their leading ideas. A greater sensitivity to individual differences need not exclude a capacity, chastened to be sure, to articulate some nearly universal insights.

Finally, given the way that over the past century or so universities have divvied up various scholarly pursuits into academic departments often characterized by distinct methodologies, the goal of finding the connections between these discrete intellectual subdivisions has been hard to reach. Catholic intellectuals need to make connections. Without such connections, there is little wisdom. Scholars of Catholic faith in the modern academy face then a special challenge: how to overcome the balkanization of knowledge typical of the modern academy, especially those universities that have doctoral programs. It might be helpful here to recall that specialization as such is not the problem; rather, fragmentation is. Some scholars need to specialize and do so without promoting needless divisions among bodies of knowledge. Mary Douglas has plunged deeply enough into her research during her long and fruitful career as an anthropologist to make all sorts of enlightening connections. Charles Taylor, recognized as a world-class philosopher, moves easily from philosophy to sociology to history and even to theology. Catholic scholars in the academy typically make connections among various disciplines.

Besides fragmentation, the modern university can make it difficult for Catholic scholars by the sometimes reductive limitations various methodologies associated with certain disciplines place upon scholars working within them. Were Catholic scholars to do their research by employing only certain already established methodologies, they would run the risk of constricting their thinking in such a way that they ask only those questions that they believe they can answer, or that they have the means to answer. In other words, as British theologian Denys Turner recently put it, they will ask only "sensible questions whose route to an answer is governed by agreed methodologies." Turner worries, as should all Catholic intellectuals, that in our universities and colleges there is the danger that "we will reverse the traffic between question and answer so as to permit only such questions to be asked as we already possess predetermined methodologies for answering, cutting the agenda of questions down to the shape and size of our given routines for answering them."[3] Were Catholic scholars to ask only such questions as they can answer, then they would not only spell the death of the disciplines as sources of wisdom, but also give us reasons why in the last analysis we would not be able to put much faith in the academy—since by the academy's own prescribed approaches to reliable knowledge, those aspects of knowing best characterized as faith would be excluded. Though the professionalization of the disciplines has in many cases improved the rigor of our research, it has done so often at the price of preventing us from posing deeper questions, and at the expense of a serious exploration of the integration of knowledge. One of the real pleasures of reading these lectures is to see how all of them make connections and ask the most profound of questions.

CATHOLIC SCHOLARS AND THE "IVORY TOWER"

Do academics really live in an "ivory tower," a place with a rarified atmosphere far removed from the real world? When in colloquial English we say that something is "academic," we mean that it has little importance. If these characterizations are accurate, nothing should help keep Catholic scholars from becoming merely "academic" more than their Catholic faith. Catholic intellectual traditions are rooted in beliefs and practices which include in their scope and outreach all of humanity and all of creation.

Consider first foundational Catholic teachings. The doctrine of creation affirms that all that is good is good because it is from God.

Moreover, all human beings are created in the image and likeness of God, an image whose dignity is made clearest in the person of Jesus Christ, the human face of God. But Jesus, though fully human and divine, is not all of God. Catholics also affirm, with other Christians, the existence of the Trinity: Father, Son, and Holy Spirit. The Christian godhead is a community of persons. Catholic Christians build community through the sacraments, primarily through the Eucharist. All who believe are invited to that sacred table.

Consider also the practices. Building community, the breaking of the bread, and the laying down of one's life for others are paradigmatic practices for Christians. A sacramental vision, drawing upon personal discipline, selfless sacrifice, and genuine thanks, reveals God's presence in our midst and in the "other" as well. Catholics are saved, not by faith alone, but also by the works that faith equips us to perform—extending ourselves and our resources to those less fortunate, exposing injustices wherever they are found, speaking the truth to power, and doing all this because of a great love for God and one another.

These teachings and practices demand a great deal from Catholic intellectuals. They also make it less likely that Catholic intellectuals will live in ivory towers. Consider the power of Gustavo Gutiérrez's passionate call that we take seriously to heart the cry of the poor. "The Lord hears the cry of the poor," a phrase sung often as a responsorial psalm at the celebration of the Eucharist. Gutiérrez asks if all Catholics hear that cry as the Lord does.

Catholic beliefs and practices locate scholarly research and teaching in a communal search for the truth and a lifelong dedication to the common good. The education Catholic scholars offer should not be about students deciding who they want to be, but rather students discovering who they have been called to be. More important than the question of identity is realizing to whom we belong. And such a discovery is not a passive acceptance of a divine given, but rather the discovery of a vocation that invites persons to lay down their lives for others. To cite Mark Roche, Catholicism insures that research and teaching will have a strong existential component:

> At a Catholic university students pursue theology not as the disinterested science of religious phenomena but as faith seeking under-

standing. They study history and the classics in order to learn not simply *about* the past, but also *from* the past. Students employ the quantitative tools of the social sciences not simply as a formal exercise with mathematical models but in order to develop sophisticated responses to pressing and complex social issues.[4]

Though having spent most of their lives outside of the academy, Margaret O'Brien Steinfels and Peter Steinfels have all their lives tackled issues of existential import, not just for the Catholic community, but everyone else as well. Mary Ann Glendon studies the origins after World War II of the concept of human rights. Mary Douglas studies ancient societies and ancient writings—a study that is useful in itself—but in that process illuminates the structures that today can make life more livable for everyone. Charles Taylor both critiques "modernity" as well as sees within it new emphases that will, if properly understood and directed, benefit everyone. Cardinal Dulles's description of his role as a theologian clearly benefits all believers and all who seek to be believers. Jill Ker Conway underscores the dignity of every person, and particularly the importance of recognizing the distinctive voices of those most likely to live in silence. Marcia Colish settles for nothing less than full freedom to search for the truth of things so that all people might acquire a better understanding of life and history, and indeed of their own religious beliefs. And finally, Gustavo Gutiérrez presents to all who are so privileged as to be scholars the challenge to respond to the needs of the poor.

Each of the Catholic scholars in this volume dwells not in an ivory tower but rather in a community of existential concern. Their interests are not antiquarian and their perspectives are not cynical. They are great teachers because they have learned much, and the part they play in the academy and beyond enriches us all.

CHAPTER I

A Catholic Modernity?

CHARLES TAYLOR

I want to say first how deeply honored I am to have been chosen as this year's recipient of the Marianist Award. I am very grateful to the University of Dayton, not only for their recognition of my work, but also for this chance to raise today with you some issues which have been at the center of my concern for decades. They have been reflected in my philosophical work, but not in the same form as I raise them this afternoon, because of the nature of philosophical discourse (as I see it, anyway), which has to try to persuade honest thinkers of any and all metaphysical or theological commitments. I am very glad of the chance to open out with you some of the questions which surround the notion of a catholic modernity.

I

My title could have been reversed; I could have called this talk: "a modern catholicism?" But such is the force of this adjective "modern" in our culture, that one might immediately get the sense that the object of my search was a new, better, higher catholicism, meant to replace all those outmoded varieties which clutter up our past. But to search for this would be to chase a chimera, a monster that cannot exist in the nature of things.

Cannot exist because of what "Catholicism" means, at least to me. So I'll start saying a word about that. "Go ye and teach all nations." How to understand this injunction? The easy way, the one in which it has all too often been taken, has been to take the global worldview of us who are Christians, and strive to make over other nations and cultures to fit it. But this violates one of the basic demands of Catholicism. I want to take the original word *katholou* in two related senses, comprising both universality and wholeness; one might say: universality through wholeness.

Redemption happens through Incarnation, the weaving of God's life into human lives. But these human lives are different, plural, irreducible to each other. Redemption-Incarnation brings reconciliation, a kind of oneness. But this is the oneness of diverse beings who come to see that they cannot attain wholeness alone, that their complementarity is essential, rather than of beings who come to accept that they are ultimately identical. Or perhaps we might put it: complementarity and identity will both be part of our ultimate oneness. Our great historical temptation has been to forget the complementarity, to go straight for the sameness, making as many people as possible into "good catholics"—and in the process failing of catholicity.

Failing of catholicity, because failing wholeness: unity bought at the price of suppressing something of the diversity in the humanity that God created; unity of the part masquerading as the whole. Universality without wholeness, and so not true catholicism.

This unity-across-difference, as against unity-through-identity, seems the only one possible for us, not only because of the diversity among humans, starting with the difference between men and women, and ramifying outward. It's not just that the human material, with which God's life is to be interwoven, imposes this formula, as a kind of second-best solution to sameness. Nor is it just because any unity between humans and God would have to be one across (immense) difference. But it seems that the life of God itself, understood as trinitarian, is already a oneness of this kind. Human diversity is part of the way in which we are made in the image of God.

So a Catholic principle, if I can put it in this perhaps over-rigid way, is: no widening of the faith without an increase in the variety of devotions and spiritualities and liturgical forms and responses to Incarnation. This is a demand which we in the Catholic Church have often failed to respect, but which we have also often tried to live up to—I'm thinking, for instance, of the great Jesuit missions in China and India at the beginning of the modern era.

The advantage of us moderns is that, living in the wake of so many varied forms of Christian life, we have this vast field of spiritualities already there before us with which to compensate for our own narrowness, to remind us of all that we need to complement our own partiality, on our road to wholeness. Which is why I'm chary of the possible resonance of "a modern catholicism" with the potential echoes of triumphalism and self-sufficiency residing in the adjective (added to those which have often enough resided in the noun)!

The point is not to be a "modern catholic," if by this we (perhaps semiconsciously and surreptitiously) begin to see ourselves as the ultimate "compleat catholics," summing up and going beyond our less advantaged ancestors[1] (a powerful connotation which hangs over the word "modern" in much contemporary use). The point rather is, taking our modern civilization for another of those great cultural forms which have come and gone in human history, to see what it means to be a Christian here, to find our authentic voice in the eventual catholic chorus; to try to do for our time and place what Mateo Ricci was striving to do four centuries ago in China.

I realize how strange, even outlandish, it seems to take Mateo Ricci and the great Jesuit experiment in China as our model here. It seems impossible to take this kind of stance toward our time; and that for two opposite reasons. First, we are too close to it. This is still, in many respects, a Christian civilization; at least, it is a society with many churchgoers. How can we start from the outsider's standpoint which was inevitably Ricci's?

But immediately as we say this, we are reminded of all those facets of modern thought and culture which strive to define Christian faith as the other, as what needs to be overcome and set firmly in the past, if Enlightenment, liberalism, humanism is to flourish. With this in mind, it's not hard to feel an outsider. But just for this reason, the Ricci project can seem totally inappropriate. He faced another civilization, one built largely in ignorance of the Judeo-Christian revelation; so the question could arise how to adapt this latter to these new addressees. But to see modernity under its non-Christian aspect is generally to see it as anti-Christian, as deliberately excluding the Christian kerygma. And how can you adapt your message to its negation?

So the Ricci project in relation to our own time looks strange for two seemingly incompatible reasons. On one hand, we feel already at home here, in this civilization which has issued from Christendom, so what do we need to strive further to understand? On the other hand, whatever is foreign to Christianity seems to involve a rejection of it, so how can we envisage accommodating? Put in other terms, the Ricci project involves the difficult task of making new discriminations: what in the culture represents a valid human difference, and what is incompatible with Christian faith? The celebrated debate about the Chinese rites turned on this issue. But it seems that for modernity, things are already neatly sorted out: whatever is in continuity with our past is legitimate Christian culture, and the novel, secularist twist to things is simply incompatible. No further enquiry seems necessary.

Now I think that this double reaction, which we are easily tempted to go along with, is quite wrong. The view I'd like to defend, if I can put it in a nutshell, is that in modern, secularist culture there are mingled together both authentic developments of the Gospel, of an Incarnational mode of life, and also a closing off to God which negates the Gospel. The notion is that modern culture, in breaking with the structures and beliefs of Christendom, also carried certain facets of Christian life further than they ever were taken, or could have been taken within Christendom. In relation to the earlier forms of Christian culture, we have to face the humbling realization that the breakout was a necessary condition of the development.

For instance, modern liberal political culture is characterized by an affirmation of universal human rights—to life, freedom, citizenship, self-realization—which are seen as radically unconditional. That is, they are not dependent on such things as gender, cultural belonging, civilizational development, or religious allegiance, which always limited them in the past. As long as we were living within the terms of "Christendom," that is, of a civilization where the structures, institutions, and culture were all supposed to reflect the Christian nature of the society (even in the nondenominational form in which this was understood in the early United States), we could never have attained this radical unconditionality. It is difficult for a "Christian" society, in this sense, to accept full equality of rights for atheists, or people of a quite alien religion, or those who violate what seems to be the Christian moral code (e.g., homosexuals).

This is not because having Christian faith as such makes you narrow or intolerant, as many militant unbelievers say. We have our share of bigots and zealots, to be sure, but we are far from alone in this. The record of certain forms of militant atheism in this century is far from reassuring. No, the impossibility I was arguing for doesn't lie in Christian faith itself, but in the project of Christendom: the attempt to marry the faith with a form of culture and a mode of society. There is something noble in the attempt; indeed, it is inspired by the very logic of Incarnation I mentioned above, whereby it strives to be interwoven more and more in human life. But as a project to be realized in history, it is ultimately doomed to frustration; it even threatens to turn into its opposite.

That's because human society in history inevitably involves coercion (as political society, at least, but also in other ways); it involves the pressure of conformity; it involves inescapably some confiscation of the highest ideals for narrow interests; and a host of other imperfections. There can never be a total fusion of the faith and any particular society; and the attempt to achieve it is dangerous for the faith. Something of this kind has been recognized from the beginning of Christianity in the distinction between church and state. The various constructions of Christendom since then could be seen unkindly as attempts post-Constantine to bring Christianity closer to the other, prevalent forms of religion, where the sacred was bound up with and supported the political order. A lot more can be said for the project of Christendom than this unfavorable judgment allows. But nevertheless, this project at its best sails very close to the wind, and is in constant danger of turning into a parodic denial of itself.

Thus to say that the fullness of rights culture couldn't have come about under Christendom is not to point to a special weakness of Christian faith. Indeed, the attempt to put some secular philosophy in the place of the faith—Jacobinism, Marxism—has scarcely led to better results (and in some cases, spectacularly worse). This culture has flourished where the casing of Christendom has been broken open, and where no other single philosophy has taken its place, but the public sphere has remained the locus of competing ultimate visions.

I also make no assumption that modern rights culture is perfectly all right as it is. On the contrary, it has lots of problems. I hope to come to some of these later. But for all its drawbacks, it has produced something quite remarkable: the attempt to call political power to book against a yardstick of fundamental human requirements, universally applied. As John Paul II has amply testified, it is impossible for the Christian conscience not to be moved by this.

This example illustrates the thesis I'm trying to argue here. Somewhere along the line of the last centuries the Christian faith was attacked from within Christendom and dethroned. In some cases, gradually dethroned, without being frontally attacked (largely in Protestant countries); but this displacement also often meant sidelining, rendering the faith irrelevant to great segments of modern life. In other cases, the confrontation was bitter, even violent; the dethroning followed long and vigorous attack (e.g., in France, in Spain, that is, largely in Catholic countries). In neither case is the development particularly comforting for Christian faith. And yet, we have to agree that it was this process which made possible what we now recognize as a great advance in the practical penetration of the Gospel in human life.

Where does this leave us? Well, it's a humbling experience. But also a liberating one. The humbling side: we are reminded by our more aggressive secularist colleagues: "It's lucky that the show is no longer being run by you card-carrying Christians, or we'd be back with the Inquisition." The liberating side comes when we recognize the truth in this (however exaggerated the formulation), and draw the appropriate conclusions. This kind of freedom, so much the fruit of the Gospel, we have only when nobody (that is, no particular outlook) is running the show. So a vote of thanks to Voltaire and others for (not necessarily wittingly) showing us this, and allowing us to live the Gospel in a purer way, free of that continual and often bloody forcing of conscience which was the sin and blight of all those "Christian" centuries. The Gospel was always meant to stand out, unencumbered by arms. We have now been able to return a little closer to this ideal—with a little help from our enemies.

Does acknowledging our debt mean that we have to fall silent? Not at all. This freedom, which is prized by so many different people for different reasons, also has its Christian meaning. It is, for instance, the freedom to come to God on one's own; or otherwise put, moved only by the Holy Spirit, whose barely audible voice will often be heard better when the loudspeakers of armed authority are silent.

That is true, but it may well be that Christians will feel reticent about articulating this meaning, lest they be seen as trying to take over again, by giving the (authoritative) meaning. But here they may be doing a disservice to this freedom. And this for a reason which they are far from being alone in seeing, but which they are often more likely to discern than their secularist compatriots.

The very fact that freedom has been well served by a situation in which no view is in charge, that it has therefore gained from the relative weakening of Christianity, and from the absence of any other strong, transcendental outlook, can seem to accredit the view that human life is better off without transcendental vision altogether. The development of modern freedom is then identified with the rise of an exclusive humanism, that is, one based exclusively on a notion of human flourishing, which recognizes no valid aim beyond this. The strong sense which continually arises that there is something more, that human life aims beyond itself, is stamped as an illusion; and judged to be a dangerous illusion, since the peaceful coexistence of people in freedom has already been identified as the fruit of waning transcendental visions.

To a Christian, this outlook seems stifling. Do we really have to pay this price to enjoy modern freedom? A kind of spiritual lobotomy? Well, no one can deny that religion generates dangerous passions. But that is far from being the whole story. Exclusive humanism also carries great dangers, which remain very underexplored in modern thought.

II

I want to look at two of these here. In doing so, I will be offering my own interpretation of modern life and sensibilities. All this is very much open to contestation. But we urgently need new perspectives in this domain, as it were, Ricci-readings of modernity.

The first danger that threatens an exclusive humanism, which wipes out the transcendent beyond life, is that it provokes as reaction an immanent negation of life. Let me try to explain this a little better.

I have been speaking of the transcendent as being "beyond life." In doing this, I am trying to get at something which is essential not only in Christianity, but in a number of other faiths, for instance, in Buddhism. A fundamental idea enters these faiths in very different forms, an idea which one might try to grasp in the claim that life isn't the whole story.

There is one way to take this expression, which is as meaning something like: life goes on after death; there is a continuation; our life doesn't totally end in our deaths. I don't mean to deny what is affirmed on this reading, but I want to take the expression here in a somewhat different (though undoubtedly related) sense.

What I mean is something more like: the point of things isn't exhausted by life, the fullness of life, even the goodness of life. This is not meant to be just a repudiation of egoism, the idea that the fullness of my life (and perhaps those of people I love) should be my concern. Let us agree with John Stuart Mill that a full life must involve striving for the benefit of humankind. Then acknowledging the transcendent means seeing a point beyond that.

One form of this is the insight that we can find in suffering and death not merely negation, the undoing of fullness and life, but also a place to affirm something which matters beyond life, on which life itself originally draws. The last clause seems to bring us back into the focus on life. It may be readily understandable even within the purview of an exclusive humanism how one could accept suffering and death in order to give life to others. On a certain view, that too has been part of the fullness of life. Acknowledging the transcendent involves something more. What matters beyond life doesn't matter just because it sustains life; otherwise it wouldn't be "beyond life" in the meaning of the act. (For Christians, God wills human flourishing, but "thy will be done" doesn't reduce to "let human beings flourish.")

This is the way of putting it which goes most against the grain of contemporary Western civilization. There are other ways of framing it. One which goes back to the very beginning of Christianity is a redefinition of the term "life" to incorporate what I'm calling "beyond life": for instance, the NewTestament evocations of "eternal life," and John 10:10.

Or we could put it in a third way: acknowledging the transcendent means being called to a change of identity. Buddhism gives us an obvious reason to talk this way. The change here is quite radical, from self to "no-self" (*anatta*). But Christian faith can be seen in the same terms: as calling for a radical decentering of the self, in relation with God. ("Thy will be done.") In the language of Abbé Henri Bremond in his magnificent study of French seventeenth-century spiritualities,[2] we can speak of "theocentrism." This way of putting it brings out a similar point to my first way, since most conceptions of a flourishing life assume a stable identity, the self for whom flourishing can be defined.

So acknowledging the transcendent means aiming beyond life, or opening yourself to a change in identity. But if you do this, where do you stand to human flourishing? There is much division, confusion, uncertainty about this. Historic religions have in fact combined concern for flourishing and transcendence in their normal practice. It has even been the rule that the supreme achievements of those who went beyond life have served to nourish the fullness of life of those who remain on this side of the barrier. Thus prayers at the tombs of martyrs brought long life, health, and a whole host of good things for the Christian faithful. Something of the same is true for the tombs of certain saints in Muslim lands; while in Theravada Buddhism, for example, the dedication of monks is turned, through blessings, amulets, etc., to all the ordinary purposes of flourishing among the laity.

Over against this, there have recurrently been "reformers" in all religions who have considered this symbiotic, complementary relation between renunciation and flourishing to be a travesty. They insist on returning religion to its "purity," and posit the goals of renunciation on their own, as goals for everyone, and disintricated from the pursuit of flourishing. Some are even moved to denigrate the latter pursuit altogether, to declare it unimportant, or an obstacle to sanctity.

But this extreme stance runs athwart a very central thrust in some religions. Christianity and Buddhism will be my examples here. Renouncing, aiming beyond life, not only takes you away, but also brings you back to flourishing. In Christian terms, if renunciation decenters you in relation with God, God's will is that humans flourish, and so you are taken back to an affirmation of this flourishing, which is biblically called *agapê*. In Buddhist terms, Enlightenment doesn't just turn you from the world, but also opens the floodgates of *metta* (loving kindness) and *karuna* (compassion). There is the Theravada concept of the Paccekabuddha, concerned only for his own salvation, but he is ranked below the highest Buddha, who acts for the liberation of all beings.

Thus outside of the stance which accepts the complementary symbiosis of renunciation and flourishing, and beyond the stance of purity, there is a third one, which I could call the stance of agapê/*karuna*.

Enough has been said to bring out the conflict between modern culture and the transcendent. In fact, a powerful constitutive strand of modern Western spirituality is involved in an affirmation of life. It is perhaps evident in the contemporary concern to preserve life, to bring prosperity, to reduce suffering, worldwide, which is, I believe, without precedent in history.

This arises historically out of what I have called elsewhere[3] "the affirmation of ordinary life." What I was trying to gesture at with this term is the cultural revolution of the early modern period, which dethroned the supposedly higher activities of contemplation and the citizen life, and put the center of gravity of goodness in ordinary living, production and the family. It belongs to this spiritual outlook that our first concern ought to be to increase life, relieve suffering, foster prosperity. Concern above all for the "good life" smacked of pride, of self-absorption. And beyond that, it was inherently inegalitarian, since the alleged "higher" activities could only be carried out by an élite minority, whereas leading rightly one's ordinary life was open to everyone. This is a moral temper to which it seems obvious that our major concern must be our dealings with others, injustice and benevolence; and these dealings must be on a level of equality.

This affirmation, which constitutes a major component of our modern ethical outlook, was originally inspired by a mode of Christian piety. It exalted practical agapê, and was polemically directed against the pride, élitism, one might say self-absorption, of those who believed in "higher" activities or spiritualities.

Consider the Reformers' attack on the supposedly "higher" vocations of the monastic life. These were meant to mark out élite paths of superior dedication, but were in fact deviations into pride and self-delusion. The really holy life for the Christian was within ordinary life itself, living in work and household in a Christian and worshipful manner.

There was an earthly, one might say earthy, critique of the allegedly "higher" here which was then transposed, and used as a secular critique of Christianity, and indeed, religion in general. Something of the same rhetorical stance adopted by Reformers against monks and nuns is taken up by secularists and unbelievers against Christian faith itself. This allegedly scorns the real, sensual, earthly human good for some purely imaginary higher end, the pursuit of which can only lead to the frustration of the real, earthly good, to suffering, mortification, repression, etc. The motivations of those who espouse this "higher" path are thus, indeed, suspect. Pride, élitism, and the desire to dominate play a part in this story too, along with fear and timidity (also present in the earlier Reformers' story, but less prominent).

In this critique, of course, religion is identified with the second, purist stance above, or else with a combination of this and the first "symbiotic" (usually labeled "superstitious") stance. The third, the stance of *agapê/karuna*, becomes invisible. That is because a transformed variant of it has in fact been assumed by the secularist critic.

Now one mustn't exaggerate. This outlook on religion is far from being universal in our society. One might think that this is particularly true in the United States, with the high rates here of religious belief and practice. And yet, I want to claim that this whole way of understanding things has penetrated far deeper and wider than simply card-carrying, village-atheist-style secularists, that it also shapes the outlook of many people who see themselves as believers.

What do I mean by "this way of understanding?" Well, it is a climate of thought, a horizon of assumptions, more than a doctrine. That means that there will be some distortion in the attempt to lay it out in a set of propositions. But I'm going to do that anyway, because there is no other way of characterizing it that I know.

If it were spelled out in propositions, it would read something like this: (*a*) that for us life, flourishing, driving back the frontiers of death and suffering are of supreme value; (*b*) that this wasn't always so; it wasn't so for our ancestors, and for people in other earlier civilizations; (*c*) that one of the things which stopped it being so in the past was precisely a sense, inculcated by religion, that there were "higher" goals; (*d*) that we have arrived at *a* by a critique and overcoming of (this kind of) religion.

We live in something analogous to a postrevolutionary climate. Revolutions generate the sense that they have won a great victory, and identify the adversary in the previous régime. A postrevolutionary climate is one which is extremely sensitive to anything which smacks of the ancien régime, and sees backsliding even in relatively innocent concessions to generalized human preferences. Thus, Puritans who saw the return of popery in any rituals, or Bolsheviks who compulsively addressed people as "Comrade," proscribing the ordinary appellation "Mister."

I would argue that a milder, but very pervasive version of this kind of climate is widespread in our culture. To speak of aiming beyond life is to appear to undermine the supreme concern with life of our humanitarian, "civilized" world. It is to try to reverse the revolution, and bring back the bad old order of priorities, in which life and happiness could be sacrificed on the altars of renunciation. Hence, even believers are often induced to redefine their faith in such a way as not to challenge the primacy of life.

My claim is that this climate, often unaccompanied by any formulated awareness of the underlying reasons, pervades our culture. It emerges, for instance, in the widespread inability to give any human meaning to suffering and death, other than as dangers and enemies to be avoided or combatted. This inability is not just the failing of certain individuals; it is entrenched in many of our institutions and practices, for instance the practice of medicine, which has great trouble understanding its own limits, or conceiving some natural term to human life.[4]

What gets lost, as always, in this postrevolutionary climate is the crucial nuance. Challenging the primacy can mean two things. It can mean trying to displace the saving of life and the avoidance of suffering from their rank as central concerns of policy. Or it can also mean making the claim, or at least opening the way for the insight, that more than life matters. These two are evidently not the same. It is not even true, as people might plausibly believe, that they are causally linked, in the sense that making the second challenge "softens us up," and makes the first challenge easier. Indeed, I want to claim (and did in the concluding chapter of *Sources*) that the reverse is the case: that clinging to the primacy of life in the second (let's call this the "metaphysical") sense is making it harder for us to affirm it wholeheartedly in the first (or practical) sense.

But I don't want to pursue this claim right now. I return to it below. The thesis I'm presenting here is that it is in virtue of its "postrevolutionary climate" that Western modernity is very inhospitable to the transcendent. This, of course, runs contrary to the mainline Enlightenment story, according to which religion has become less credible thanks to the advance of science. There is, of course, something in this, but it isn't in my view the main story. More, to the extent that it is true, that is, that people interpret science and religion as at loggerheads, it is often because of an already felt incompatibility at the moral level. It is this deeper level that I have been trying to explore here.

In other words, to oversimplify again, the obstacles to belief in Western modernity are primarily moral and spiritual, rather than epistemic. I am talking about the driving force here, rather than what is said in justification of unbelief in arguments.

III

But I am in danger of wandering from the main line of my argument. I have been painting a portrait of our age in order to be able to suggest that exclusive humanism has provoked, as it were, a revolt from within. But before I do this, let us pause to notice how in the secularist affirmation of ordinary life, just as with the positing of universal and unconditional rights, an undeniable prolongation of the Gospel has been perplexingly linked with a denial of transcendence.

We live in an extraordinary moral culture, measured against the norm of human history, in which suffering and death, through famine, flood, earthquake, pestilence, or war, can awaken worldwide movements of sympathy and practical solidarity. Granted, of course, that this is made possible by modern media and modes of transportation, not to speak of surpluses. These shouldn't blind us to the importance of the cultural-moral change. The same media and means of transport don't awaken the same response everywhere; it is disproportionately strong in ex-Latin Christendom.

Let us grant also the distortions produced by media hype and the media-gazer's short attention span, the way dramatic pictures produce the strongest response, often relegating even more needy cases to a zone of neglect from which only the cameras of CNN can rescue them. Nevertheless, the phenomenon is remarkable, and for the Christian conscience inspiring. The age of Hiroshima and Auschwitz has also produced Amnesty International and Médecins sans Frontières.

The Christian roots of all this run deep. First, there is the extraordinary missionary effort of the Counter-Reformation church, taken up later by the Protestant denominations. Then there were the mass-mobilization campaigns of the early nineteenth century—the antislavery movement in England, largely inspired and led by Evangelicals; the parallel abolitionist movement in this country, also largely Christian inspired. Then this habit of mobilizing for the redress of injustice and the relief of suffering worldwide becomes part of our political culture. Somewhere along the road, this culture ceases to be simply Christian inspired—although people of deep Christian faith continue to be important in today's movements. Moreover, it needed this breach with the culture of Christendom, as I argued above in connection with human rights, for the impulse of solidarity to transcend the frontier of Christendom itself.

So we see a phenomenon, of which the Christian conscience cannot but say "flesh of my flesh, and bone of my bone," and which is paradoxically often seen by some of its most dedicated carriers as conditional on a denial of the transcendent. We return again to the point our argument was at some time ago, in which the Christian conscience experiences a mixture of humility and unease—the humility in realizing that the break with Christendom was necessary for this great extension of Gospel-inspired actions; the unease in the sense that the denial of transcendence places this action under threat.

Which bring us back to the main line of the argument. One such threat is what I am calling the immanent revolt. Of course this is not something that can be demonstrated beyond doubt to those who don't see it. And yet, from another perspective, it is just terribly obvious. I am going to offer a perspectival reading. In the end we have to ask ourselves which perspective makes the most sense of human life.

Exclusive humanism closes the transcendent window, as though there were nothing beyond—more, as though it weren't a crying need of the human heart to open that window, and first gaze, then go beyond. As though feeling this need were the result of a mistake, an erroneous worldview, bad conditioning, or worse, some pathology. Two radically different perspectives on the human condition. Who is right?

Well, who can make more sense of the life all of us are living? If we are right, then human beings have an ineradicable bent to respond to something beyond life. Denying this stifles. But then, even for those who accept the metaphysical primacy of life, this outlook will itself seem imprisoning.

Now there is a feature of modern culture which fits this perspective. This is the revolt from within unbelief, as it were, against the primacy of life. Not now in the name of something beyond, but really more just from a sense of being confined, diminished by the acknowledgment of this primacy. This has been an important stream in our culture, something woven into the inspiration of poets, and writers—for example, Baudelaire (but was he entirely an unbeliever?) and Mallarmé. But the most influential proponent of this kind of view is undoubtedly Nietzsche. And it is significant that the most important antihumanist thinkers of our time—for example, Foucault, Derrida, and behind them, Bataille—all draw heavily on Nietzsche.

Nietzsche, of course, rebelled against the idea that our highest goal is to preserve and increase life, to prevent suffering. He rejects this both metaphysically and practically. He rejects the egalitarianism underlying this whole affirmation of ordinary life. But his rebellion is in a sense also internal. Life itself can push to cruelty, to domination, to exclusion, and indeed does so in its moments of most exuberant affirmation.

So this move remains within the modern affirmation of life in a sense. There is nothing higher than the movement of life itself (the Will to Power). But it chafes at the benevolence, the universalism, the harmony, the order. It wants to rehabilitate destruction and chaos, the infliction of suffering and exploitation, as part of the life to be affirmed. Life properly understood also affirms death and destruction. To pretend otherwise is to try to restrict it, tame it, hem it in, deprive it of its highest manifestations, what makes it something you can say yes to.

A religion of life which would proscribe death-dealing, the infliction of suffering, is confining and demeaning. Nietzsche thinks of himself as having taken up some of the legacy of pre-Platonic and pre-Christian warrior ethics, their exaltation of courage, greatness, élite excellence. Modern life-affirming humanism breeds pusillanimity. This accusation frequently occurs in the culture of counter-Enlightenment.

Of course, one of the fruits of this counterculture was Fascism—to which Nietzsche's influence was not entirely foreign, however true and valid is Walter Kaufman's refutation of the simple myth of Nietzsche as a proto-Nazi. But in spite of this, the fascination with death and violence recurs, for example, in the interest in Bataille, shared by Derrida and Foucault. James Miller's book on Foucault shows the depths of this rebellion against "humanism," as a stifling, confining space one has to break out of.[5]

My point here is not to score off neo-Nietzscheanism as some kind of antechamber to Fascism. A secular humanist might want to do this. But my perspective is rather different. I see these connections as another manifestation of our (human) inability to be content simply with an affirmation of life.

The Nietzschean understanding of enhanced life, which can fully affirm itself, also in a sense takes us beyond life; and in this it is analogous with other, religious notions of enhanced life (like the New Testament's "eternal life"). But it takes us beyond by incorporating a fascination with the negation of life, with death and suffering. It doesn't acknowledge some supreme good beyond life, and in that sense sees itself rightly as utterly antithetical to religion.

I am tempted to speculate further, and to suggest that the perennial human susceptibility to be fascinated by death and violence is at base a manifestation of our nature as *homo religiosus*. From the point of view of someone who acknowledges transcendence, it is one of the places this aspiration beyond most easily goes when it fails to take us there. This doesn't mean that religion and violence are simply alternatives. On the contrary, it has meant that most historical religion has been deeply intricated with violence, from human sacrifice down to intercommunal massacres. Because most historical religion remains only very imperfectly oriented to the beyond. The religious affinities of the cult of violence in its different forms are indeed palpable.

What it might mean, however, is that the only way fully to escape the draw toward violence lies somewhere in the turn to transcendence, that is, through the full-hearted love of some good beyond life. A thesis of this kind has been put forward by René Girard, for whose work I have a great deal of sympathy, although I don't agree on the centrality he gives to the scapegoat phenomenon.[6]

On the perspective I'm developing here, no position can be set aside as simply devoid of insight. We could think of modern culture as the scent of a three-cornered—perhaps ultimately, a four-cornered—battle. There are secular humanists, there are neo-Nietzscheans, and there are those who acknowledge some good beyond life. Any pair can gang up against the third on some important issue. Neo-Nietzscheans and secular humanists together condemn religion and reject any good beyond life. But neo-Nietzscheans and acknowledgers of transcendence are together in their absence of surprise at the continued disappointments of secular humanism, together also in the sense that its vision of life lacks a dimension. In a third lineup, secular humanists and believers come together in defending an idea of the human good, against the antihumanism of Nietzsche's heirs.

A fourth party can be introduced to this field if we take account of the fact that the acknowledgers of transcendence are divided. Some think that the whole move to secular humanism was just a mistake, which needs to be undone. We need to return to an earlier view of things. Others, among whom I place myself, think that the practical primacy of life has been a great gain for humankind, and that there is some truth in the "revolutionary" story: this gain was in fact unlikely to come about without some breach with established religion. (We might even be tempted to say that modern unbelief is providential, but that might be too provocative a way of putting it.) But we nevertheless think that the metaphysical primacy of life is wrong, and stifling, and that its continued dominance puts in danger the practical primacy.

I have rather complicated the scene in the last paragraphs. Nevertheless, the simple lines sketched earlier still stand out, I believe. Both secular humanists and antihumanists concur in the "revolutionary" story; that is, they see us as having been liberated from the illusion of a good beyond life, and thus enabled to affirm ourselves. This may take the form of an Enlightenment endorsement of benevolence and justice; or it may be the charter for the full affirmation of the will to power—or "the free play of the signifier," or the aesthetics of the self, or whatever the current version is. But it remains within the same postrevolutionary climate. For those fully within this climate, transcendence becomes all but invisible.

IV

The above picture of modern culture, seen from one perspective, suggests a way in which the denial of transcendence can put the most valuable gains of modernity in danger, here the primacy of rights and the affirmation of life. This is, I repeat, one perspective among others; the issue is whether it makes more sense of what has been happening over the last two centuries than that of an exclusive, secular humanism. It seems very much to me that it does so.

I want now to take up this danger from another angle. I spoke above about an immanent revolt against the affirmation of life. Nietzsche has become an important figure in the articulation of this, a counter-belief to the modern philanthropy which strives to increase life and relieve suffering. But Nietzsche also articulated something equally disquieting; an acid account of the sources of this modern philanthropy, of the mainsprings of this compassion and sympathy which powers the impressive enterprises of modern solidarity.

Nietzsche's "genealogy" of modern universalism, of the concern for the relief of suffering, of "pity," will probably not convince anyone who has the highest examples of Christian agapê, or Buddhist *karuna*, before their eyes. But the question remains very much open, whether this unflattering portrait doesn't capture the possible fate of a culture which has aimed higher than its moral sources can sustain it.

This is the issue I raised very briefly in the last chapter of *Sources*. The more impressed one is with this colossal extension of a Gospel ethic to a universal solidarity, to a concern for human beings on the other side of the globe whom we shall never meet or need as companions or compatriots; or, because that is not the ultimately difficult challenge, the more impressed we are at the sense of justice we can still feel for people we do have contact with, and tend to dislike or despise, or at a willingness to help people who often seem to be the cause of their own suffering. The more we contemplate all this, the more surprise we can feel at people generating the motivation to engage in these enterprises of solidarity, of international philanthropy, of the modern welfare state. Or to bring out the negative side, the less surprised one is when the motivation to keep them going flags, as we see in the present hardening of feeling against the impoverished and disfavored in Western democracies.

We could put the matter this way. Our age makes higher demands of solidarity and benevolence on people today than ever before. Never before have people been asked to stretch out so far, and so consistently, so systematically, so much as a matter of course, to the stranger outside the gates. A similar point can be made, if we look at the other dimension of the affirmation of ordinary life, that concerned with universal justice. Here too, we are asked to maintain standards of equality which cover wider and wider classes of people, bridge more and more kinds of difference, impinge more and more in our lives. How do we manage to do it?

Or perhaps we don't manage all that well; and the interesting and important question might run: how could we manage to do it? But at least to get close to the answer to this, we should ask: how do we do as well as we do, which after all, at first sight seems in these domains of solidarity and justice much better than in previous ages?

1. Well, one way is that performance to these standards has become part of what we understand as a decent, civilized human life. We live up to them, to the extent we do, because we would be somewhat ashamed of ourselves if we didn't. They have become part of our self-image, our sense of our own worth. And alongside this, we feel a sense of satisfaction and superiority when we contemplate others—our ancestors, or contemporary illiberal societies—who didn't or don't recognize them.

But we sense immediately how fragile this is as a motivation. It makes our philanthropy vulnerable to the shifting fashion of media attention, and the various modes of feel-good hype. We throw ourselves into the cause of the month, raise funds for this famine, petition the government to intervene in that grisly civil war; and then forget all about it next month, when it drops off the CNN screen. A solidarity ultimately driven by the giver's own sense of moral superiority is a whimsical and fickle thing. We are far in fact from the universality and unconditionality which our moral outlook prescribes.

We might envisage getting beyond this by a more exigent sense of our own moral worth; one that would require more consistency, a certain independence from fashion, careful, informed attention to the real needs. This is part of what people working in NGOs in the field must feel, who correspondingly look down on us TV-image-driven givers, as we do on the lesser breeds who don't respond to this type of campaign at all.

2. But the most exigent, lofty sense of self-worth has limitations. I feel worthy in helping people, in giving without stint. But what is worthy about helping people? It's obvious, as humans they have a certain dignity. My feelings of self-worth connect intellectually and

emotionally with my sense of the worth of human beings. Here is where modern secular humanism is tempted to congratulate itself. In replacing the low and demeaning picture of human beings as depraved, inveterate sinners, in articulating the potential of human beings for goodness and greatness, humanism has not only given us the courage to act for reform, but also explains why this philanthropic action is so immensely worthwhile. The higher the human potential, the greater the enterprise of realizing it, the more the carriers of this potential are worthy of our help in achieving it.

But philanthropy and solidarity driven by a lofty humanism, just as that which was driven often by high religious ideals, has a Janus face. On one side, in the abstract, one is inspired to act. But on the other, faced with the immense disappointments of actual human performance, with the myriad ways in which real, concrete human beings fall short of, ignore, parody, and betray this magnificent potential, one cannot but experience a growing sense of anger and futility. Are these people really worthy objects of all these efforts? Perhaps in face of all this stupid recalcitrance, it would not be a betrayal of human worth, or one's self-worth, if one abandoned them. Or perhaps the best that can be done for them is to force them to shape up.

Before the reality of human shortcomings, philanthropy—the love of the human—can gradually come to be invested with contempt, hatred, aggression. The action is broken off, or worse, continues, but invested now with these new feelings, and becomes progressively more coercive and inhumane. The history of despotic socialism, that is, twentieth-century communism, is replete with this tragic turn, brilliantly foreseen by Dostoyevsky over 100 years ago ("Starting from unlimited freedom, I arrived at unlimited despotism")[7] and then repeated again and again with a fatal regularity, through one-party régimes on a macro level, to a host of "helping" institutions on a micro level from orphanages to boarding schools for aboriginals.

The ultimate stop on the line was reached by Elena Ceaucescu in her last recorded statement before her murder by the successor régime: that the Rumanian people had shown themselves unworthy of the immense untiring efforts of her husband on their behalf.

The tragic irony is that the higher the sense of potential, the more grievously real people fall short, and the more severe the turnaround will be which is inspired by the disappointment. A lofty humanism posits high standards of self-worth, and a magnificent goal to strive toward. It inspires enterprises of great moment. But by this very token it encourages force, despotism, tutelage, ultimately contempt, and a certain ruthlessness in shaping refractory human material—oddly enough, the same horrors which Enlightenment critique picked up in societies and institutions dominated by religion.

And for the same causes. The difference of belief here is not crucial. Wherever action for high ideals is not tempered, controlled, ultimately engulfed in an unconditional love of the beneficiaries, this ugly dialectic risks repeating itself. And of course, just holding the appropriate religious beliefs is no guarantee that this will be so.

3. A third pattern of motivation, which we have seen repeatedly, this time in the register of justice rather than benevolence: we have seen it with Jacobins, Bolsheviks, and today with the politically correct left, as well as the so-called "Christian" right. We fight against injustices which cry out to heaven for vengeance. We are moved by a flaming indignation against these: racism, oppression, sexism, or leftist attacks on the family or Christian faith. This indignation comes to be fueled by hatred for those who support and connive with these injustices; and this in turn is fed by our sense of superiority that we are not like these instruments and accomplices of evil. Soon we are blinded to the havoc we wreak around us. Our picture of the world has safely located all evil outside of us. The very energy and hatred with which we combat evil proves its exteriority to us. We must never relent, but on the contrary double our energy, vie with each other in indignation and denunciation.

Another tragic irony nests here. The stronger the sense of (often correctly identified) injustice, the more powerfully this pattern can become entrenched. We become centers of hatred, generators of new modes of injustice on a greater scale, but we started with the most exquisite sense of wrong, the greatest passion for justice and equality and peace.

A Buddhist friend of mine from Thailand briefly visited the German Greens. He confessed to utter bewilderment. He thought he understood the goals of the party: peace between human beings, and a stance of respect and friendship by humans toward nature. But what astonished him was all the anger, the tone of denunciation, of hatred toward the established parties. These people didn't seem to see that the first step toward their goal would have to involve stilling the anger and aggression in themselves. He couldn't understand what they were up to.

The blindness is typical of modern exclusive secular humanism. This modern humanism prides itself on having released energy for philanthropy and reform; by getting rid of "original sin," of a lowly and demeaning picture of human nature, it encourages us to reach high. Of course, there is some truth in this. But it is also terribly partial, terribly naive, because it has never faced the questions I have been raising here: what can power this great effort at philanthropic reform? This humanism leaves us with our own high sense of self-worth to keep us from backsliding, a high notion of human worth to inspire us forward, and a flaming indignation against wrong and oppression to energize us. It cannot appreciate how problematic all of these are, how easily they can slide into something trivial, ugly or downright dangerous and destructive.

A Nietzschean genealogist can have a field day here. Nothing gave Nietzsche greater satisfaction than showing how morality or spirituality is really powered by its direct opposite—for example, that the Christian aspiration to love is really motivated by the hatred of the weak for the strong. Whatever one thinks of this judgment on Christianity, it is clear that modern humanism is full of potential for such disconcerting reversals: from dedication to others to self-indulgent, feel-good responses, from a lofty sense of human dignity to control powered by contempt and hatred, from absolute freedom to absolute despotism, from a flaming desire to help the oppressed to an incandescent hatred for all those who stand in the way. And the higher the flight, the greater the potential fall.

Perhaps after all, it's safer to have small goals, not-too-great expectations and be somewhat cynical about human potentiality from the start. This is undoubtedly so, but then one also risks not having the motivation to undertake great acts of solidarity, and combat great injustices. In the end, the question becomes a maximum one: how to have the greatest degree of philanthropic action with the minimum hope in mankind. A figure like Dr. Rieux in Camus' *La Peste* stands as a possible solution to this problem. But that is fiction. What is possible in real life?

I said earlier that just having appropriate beliefs is no solution to these dilemmas. And the transformation of high ideals into brutal practice was demonstrated lavishly in Christendom well before modern humanism came on the scene. So is there a way out?

This cannot be a matter of guarantee, only of faith. But it is clear that Christian spirituality points to one. It can be described in two ways—either as a love and compassion which is unconditional, that is, not based on what you the recipient have made of yourself; or as one based on what you are most profoundly, a being in the image of God. They obviously amount to the same thing. In either case, the love is not conditional on the worth realized in you just as an individual, or even in what is realizable in you alone. That's because being made in the image of God, as a feature of each human being, is not something that can be characterized just by reference to this being alone. Our being in the image of God is also our standing among others in the stream of love which is that facet of God's life we try to grasp, very inadequately, in speaking of the Trinity.

Now it makes a whole lot of difference whether you think this kind of love is a possibility for us humans. I think it is, but only to the extent that we open ourselves to God, which means in fact, overstepping the limits set in theory by exclusive humanisms. If one does believe that, then one has something very important to say to modern times, something that addresses the fragility of what all of us, believers and unbelievers alike, most value in these times.

Can we try to take stock of the first leg of our strange Ricci-like journey into the present? The trip is obviously not complete. We have just looked at some facets of modernity: the espousal of universal and unconditional rights, the affirmation of life, universal justice, and benevolence. Important as these are, there are plainly others: for instance, freedom; and also the ethic of authenticity,[8] to mention just two. Nor have I had time to examine other dark features of modernity, such as its drive toward instrumental reason and control. But I think an examination of these other facets would show a similar pattern. So I'd like to try to define this more closely.

In a sense our journey was a flop. Imitating Ricci would involve taking a distance from our time, feeling as strange in it as he was arriving in China. But what we saw as children of Christendom was first, something terribly familiar—certain intimations of the Gospel, carried to unprecedented lengths; and second, a flat negation of our faith—exclusive humanism. But still, like Ricci, we were bewildered by this. We had to struggle (as he did) to make a discernment. He wanted to distinguish between those things in the new culture which came from the natural knowledge we all have of God, and should be affirmed and extended, on one hand; and those practices which were distortions and would have to be changed on the other. And similarly, we are challenged to a difficult discernment, trying to see what in modern culture reflects its furthering of the Gospel, and what its refusal of the transcendent.

The point of my Ricci image is that this is not easy. And the best way to try to achieve it is to take at least some relative distance, in history if not in geography. The danger is that we not be sufficiently bewildered, that we think we have it all figured out from the start, and we know what to affirm and what to deny. We then can enter smoothly into the mainstream of a debate which is already going on in our society, about the nature and value of modernity. As I have indicated,[9] this debate tends to become polarized between "boosters" and "knockers," who either condemn or affirm modernity en bloc, thus missing what is really at stake here, which is how to rescue admirable ideals from sliding into demeaning modes of realization.

From the Christian point of view, the corresponding error is to fall into one of two untenable positions: either we pick certain fruits of modernity, like human rights, and take them on board, but then condemn the whole movement of thought and practice which underlie them, in particular the breakout from Christendom (in earlier variants, even the fruits were condemned); or in reaction to this first position, we feel we have to go all the way with the "boosters" of modernity, and become fellow travelers of exclusive humanism.

Better, I would argue, after initial (and let's face it, still continuing) bewilderment, gradually to find our voice from within the achievements of modernity; to measure the humbling degree to which some of the most impressive extensions of a Gospel ethic depended on a breakaway from Christendom; and from within these gains try to make clearer to ourselves and others the tremendous dangers that arise in them. It is perhaps not an accident that the history of the twentieth century can be read either in a perspective of progress, or in one of mounting horror. Perhaps it is not contingent that it is the century both of Auschwitz and Hiroshima, and of Amnesty International and Médicines sans Frontières. As with Ricci, the Gospel message to this time and society has to respond both to what in it already reflects the life of God, and to the doors which have been closed against this life. And in the end, it is no easier for us than it was for Ricci to discern both correctly, even if for opposite reasons. Between us twentieth-century Catholics, we have our own variants of the Chinese Rites controversy. Let us pray that we do better this time.

CHAPTER 2

The Poor and the Third Millennium

GUSTAVO GUTIÉRREZ

I would like to express my gratitude for the Marianist Award. It is a gift. We cannot refuse a gift and we never deserve it. Thus, we may only say thanks a lot. I can say this in the beautiful word we have in Spanish, "gracias." "Gracias" to this university for this gift, but also "gracias" for the presence of the Marianist people working in my continent and in my own country. I have very good friends among them.

Father Jim Heft has already announced the subject of this afternoon's lecture. I still have some difficulties expressing myself in English, but I am confident of your tolerance. In the apostolic letter *Tertio Millennio Adveniente*, Pope John Paul II invites us to celebrate a Jubilee in the year 2000. The Jubilee is a very rich and complex biblical subject directly related to the reestablishment of justice, liberation, equality, and the forgiveness of sins. In the same letter, the pope quotes chapter 4 of Luke's Gospel, a very famous text where Luke presents Jesus assuming the perspective of the Jubilee.

In turn, I would like to present to you what I think is the most important point or contribution of the Latin American church experience and its reflection in these last years, as expressed in this well-known phrase, the "preferential option for the poor." This concept was born in Latin America, and I think it is the best expression of our experience and the fruit of our reflection. The pope himself invites us to such reflection when he calls us to "an examination of conscience" on the occasion of the Jubilee. He says: "Christians must ask themselves about their responsibility for great forms of unjustice and exclusion." And he also says that in order to do it, we should put a great emphasis "on the church preferential option for the poor and the outcast" (*Tertio M.* n. 51).

I would like to reflect on this very well known disposition, this preferential option for the poor, as expressing a very important and old biblical concern. The application as such may be new, but certainly not the idea. The preferential option for the poor arises from the Bible in different ways during the history of Christianity. Maybe one simple way to discuss this question is to analyze each word, "poor," "preference," and "option."

POVERTY MEANS DEATH

When we say "option for the poor," we are thinking of the materially poor. Personally, I prefer to say the "real poor," but materially or real is quite clear. The option is for the truly poor. Therefore, we are not speaking about an option for the spiritually poor (the spiritually poor are few; it is easy to develop an option for them . . .). And what does it mean to be poor, to live in poverty? The word poverty connotes easily and rightly an economic condition of deprivation. But in any ultimate analysis, poverty means an unjust and early death. Let us make the point precisely.

Father Jim has mentioned Las Casas, who, in the sixteenth century said, "Indians are dying before their time." Unfortunately, it is still true in poor countries, like the Latin American ones, where the poor are dying before their time. They are dying early and unjustly. It is, in the ultimate analysis—I repeat—the real meaning of poverty. When I say this, I am not trying to avoid the economic dimensions of poverty; however, it is important to be clear about the roots of this poverty. I mean physical death, due to hunger or sickness. Some diseases that in developed countries have already been overcome by medical science continue to kill people in the developing ones. For example, cholera, as you may have heard, remains powerfully present among us. Recently in Latin America, starting with my own country, hundreds of people died from cholera, even though cholera has been medically overcome. It is very easy to control cholera, unless you are poor. If the poor had some economic power, we would be free of this disease, and there would be no problem because the poor are the only victims of cholera. The poor are often dying in the beginning of their lives.

But I speak not only of physical death; I also speak of a cultural one. When culture is marginalized, when we do not recognize women's human rights, in a sense we are killing them. It is not a physical assassination, but rather the destruction of very important human values that give meaning to their lives. Anthropologists love to say that culture is life. Thus, being against culture is being against life. For this reason, and to finish with this part of the notion of the poor, poverty is never good. We must be very clear about that. Please, remember that poor people may be very good ones, but real poverty is never good because it is contrary to the will of God. Poverty means death, which is contrary to the will of life of the kingdom of God. We must avoid romanticizing poverty. It is never good. We do not love poverty; we love the poor.

In addition, we must also be clear about the causes of poverty. To describe the condition of the poor is relevant, but it is not enough. In order to change the conditions of poverty, we need a structural analysis to understand its causes. If we do not understand the causes, we cannot be efficacious in our opposition to poverty. In the medical field, people speak of etiological treatment, which goes to the causes. I read many years ago, before I took an interest in liberation theology, a statement by Paul Ricoeur, a great Christian philosopher and thinker. He said, "If you are not against poverty, you are not with the poor." It is very simple but very clear. Poverty is an anti-evangelical condition. This expression comes from the Latin American bishops' conferences (Medellín, Puebla, Santo Domingo). But you know, at the same time, if you identify the causes of poverty, in that moment you risk causing trouble. People prefer only to describe poverty or to speak about the necessity of helping poor people; however, to point out the causes of poverty and overcome them is the only way to be honest to the poor.

Today the causes of poverty are not exactly the same as they were thirty years ago. Some causes are the same, but there are also several changes, because the international economy today is very different from the one of thirty years ago. The president of the Inter-American Bank of Development, Enrique Iglesias, of Uruguay, has written this short and interesting remark: "The next century will be fascinating and cruel." Indeed, *fascinating* for one part of humanity; for a lot of people in this country, the United States, for example, and for a small minority in my country of Peru. Today humanity has the capacity to change and transform nature, even beyond our planet. Many people believe this creates great possibilities. The great revolution in recent years is located in the field of knowledge. It is certainly fascinating for this reason. We know so much more. But it is *cruel* for the majority of humanity. What is fascinating for a few is cruel for the great majority of humanity because they are excluded from the realm of knowledge. In addition, people who enjoy this fascination also run the great risk of being isolated in very small groups, forming a kind of exclusive club.

In the report of the United Nations Commission for Human Development, the figures are very clear. The gap between the "haves" and the "have-nots" grows wider and wider. As Christians, we must prevent the repercussions of this situation in the next century. I think the Jubilee is a call by John Paul II to do that, recalling, for instance, one of the principles of the biblical theme of Jubilee: only God is the owner of land; that is to say, we are only administrators. It seems a very old idea, but it is a very rich one for us and for humanity today. To celebrate the Jubilee, opposing poverty is one way to avoid the cruel consequences of today.

For this reason, when the pope in his *Tertio Millennio Adveniente* speaks about the preferential option for the poor, he immediately quotes Leviticus 25, which underlines the inspiration and the theme of Jubilee, and calls for the elimination of the foreign debt that burdens so many developing countries. This is one modern application of the Jubilee. As you know better than I, the debt was paid by the poor countries a long time ago. Right now, we are paying the interests on the original amounts. My own country today pays around a billion dollars a year. Imagine the consequences if this sum could be used to satisfy the needs of our poor people. I think the elimination of foreign debt could be a clear application of the Jubilee. It is not the solution for world poverty, but it certainly removes a big obstacle today.

To conclude with the question of the poor, I do not pretend to have a good definition of the poor, but I think I have a good approach. It seems to me that the poor are the "insignificant" people. Any person is, of course, significant; but when we see people in our society who are not respected, we may say they "appear" to be insignificant. Again, depending on our economic status, our color, or our gender, we may be insignificant. The poor are the nameless people. They are anonymous during their lives and also after their death. That is what it means to be poor. The economic aspect of poverty is very important, but it is not the only one.

GOD IS THE ULTIMATE REASON OF THE PREFERENCE

I would now like to refer to the second word, "preferential." I will return to the question of the poor later. But what is the meaning of "preferential"? A frequent criticism in our time is that to show a preference is to be unfair. It could be partiality on God's part as well as on our part. For some other people, the word "preference" is too soft. Others in Latin America prefer to avoid the word "preferentila" and simply speak of an "option for the poor." I disagree because, in order to understand the meaning of this preference, we must remember the universality of the love of God. Without this proper context, we cannot understand preference. God loves everyone, without exception. This universality is very demanding because we must imitate the behavior of God and love everyone.

Only in such a framework can we speak about preference, because preference is not opposed to universality and does not mean exclusion. It means the poor are first and the others "second," but those who are second are also included. However we have, I admit, a tension between universality and preference. When we speak of preference, we are saying some people are first in my love and in my commitment, too. But if we forget the universality of God's love, preference becomes a sectarian attitude. On the other hand, if we forget preference, universality becomes very abstract, such as saying, "I love everyone," which is to say, "I really love no one."

What is the reason for this preference? The social analysis of poverty helps us to understand the concrete condition of the poor. The direct experience of poverty is very relevant. Human compassion is an important factor too, but these factors are not the ultimate reasons. The ultimate reason for the preference of the poor is the love of God; the main reason is that God is God. And God prefers the poor because they are the weakest ones, those closest to an unjust and early death. We must prefer the poor, not because *all* of them are good, but because God is good. That is the main and permanent reason. That is why the preferential option for the poor is a theocentric option, not centered in the poor, but rather in God.

Sometimes, when I lecture about this question outside of Peru or Latin America, people tell me: "I understand you very well. You are speaking so strongly about the preference for the poor because you are a Latin American." You know, my answer is always the same: "Please do not think you understand me so easily because being Latin American is not my main motivation; my main motivation is that I believe in the God of Jesus Christ."

If we take this perspective, we understand a classic point in the history of Christian spirituality. John of the Cross never spoke about social poverty, even though he was very poor and his mother at one time was a beggar. However he is very relevant for us. Why? Because John of the Cross is a person who demonstrated that God is God. And we have to say this right in the middle of our social, political, and economic commitments as Christians. God is the center of our behavior. John of the Cross recalled this with energy, so he helps us to avoid any kind of idolatry, which is a permanent risk for every Christian. In the Bible, idolatry is the temptation for every believer. For example, some people working in Latin America, sometimes without realizing it, risk making the poor into some kind of idol. It is important to avoid this idolatry, even in theology. Liberation Theology can also be a little idol for some people. However, the Bible and the saints remind us that God is the ultimate end of our commitments.

I think it is very important to be hopeful about this matter, in order to be very radical in the commitment to the poor, too. If we take seriously the preference for the poor, we may have a new approach to a very important fact today: the relation between *ethics* and the *economy*. From a Christian perspective, ethics has something to say to economics. But today, economics tries to be autonomous without relation to ethics. Economics has appropriated the model of natural science and also pretends to autonomy. This is very dangerous, I think, for people and especially for the poor. What was long considered vice becomes moral value and the virtue at the heart of liberal economy. For example, greed, avarice, and selfishness are legitimated and become good behavior because they are considered the motor of economics. In the past, however, they were considered social evils for humanity.

I want to quote a well-known British economist, Keynes. In 1930, he wrote that once the accumulation of capital is not of such great importance, we will be liberated from some pseudo-moral principles which we have accepted for two centuries since Adam Smith. In ancient times, it was possible to call things by their real names and say avarice was a vice, and love of money was awful. Keynes very lucidly wrote, "Beware, the time for all this has not arrived yet, we should wait for at least another hundred years" (that is to say, just thirty years more). "For at least another hundred years, we must pretend to ourselves, and to everyone that this fair is foul and foul is fair. For foul is useful and fair is not. Avarice and greed," Keynes continues, "must be our gods for a little longer stage, for only they can lead us out of the tunnel of economic necessity into daylight." Keynes understands well that the foundations of the neoliberal economy are immoral. But he says we "need" this immoral system for one century more. Well, it is difficult to accept this statement. I am very impressed by this text because it is very clear, very frank, and a little cynical as well.

A UNIVERSAL OPTION

I can now talk about the third word, "option." Some friends told me that maybe the word in English does not mean exactly what it means in Spanish; but at least, in both languages, option means a free decision. Some people think that only the nonpoor must espouse the option for the poor. This is not true, because this option is a universal demand. Everyone, even the poor, must undertake the option for the poor; even though many poor people have already undertaken an option for the rich. I think this option for the poor is a very demanding way of expressing an option for other people. This is very difficult to accept.

Remember the parable of the Good Samaritan. It begins with the question, "Who is my neighbor?" "My" is the possessive of I, the first person. You also remember Jesus' question: "Who of these three was the neighbor of the wounded man?" and also the answer: the other, the wounded man, was the center. To become a neighbor is a process. I need to meet someone and let that person be my neighbor and also make myself a neighbor to that person. Becoming a "neighbor" is the result of action. We must go beyond our normal path, as did the Samaritan. This is the meaning of the tale. As you well know, for many people, the poor are culturally, socially, and geographically distant; however, they should be our neighbors. We need to meet the poor and, through this approach, become their neighbors. We often think that our neighbor is nearby, the closest person; but, this is not the Gospel approach. In the Gospel, the neighbor is the one who is distant and whom I make my neighbor as a result of my action.

It seems to me that we may now be more sensitive than in the past to the situation of others. At the same time, it is difficult for many people to accept this "otherness." The poor, the insignificant, are the "others" because they are excluded from the mainstream of society. Today, we are in the process of becoming two kinds of human beings on this planet: on one hand, we have people who enjoy the majority of the resources (the haves) and, on the other, there are people who are not considered useful (the have-nots). The process is not complete, but we are definitely headed in this direction.

That is why we need an ethics of solidarity. An important Jewish philosopher, Emmanuel Levinas, has written of this matter eloquently. Based on Scripture, he states that the "other" comes first, as we saw in the parable of the Good Samaritan. For Levinas, the first philosophy is ethics, and I think it is a very demanding one. For Levinas and for Christians, the "other" is first because he or she is made in God's image. We should have the faith to recognize Jesus Christ in the face of the poor. To have a Christian perspective, we must have a very deep commitment to this ethics of solidarity. In one of the key texts in the Bible concerning Jubilee, it is written: "we must be open-handed with the poor sisters and brothers (Deut. 15)." This is exactly the idea of the Jubilee: to be open-handed, to love other people, and above all to recognize their condition as a great concern.

CONCLUSION: PREFERENTIAL OPTION FOR THE POOR AS AXIS OF CHRISTIAN LIFE

I would like to finish by returning to the title of this lecture. I have three final statements. First, the preferential option for the poor is a perspective *rooted in the Bible*. Karl Barth, a great theologian of this century, said the God of the Bible always takes sides with the lowly, the outcast, the poor. He said this not because he was reading a liberation theologian, but because he was reading the Bible and that was enough for him. We don't need to read liberation theology to learn this. It is in the core of the Christian message. You may ask why this expression, which today is so relevant, was not used before. Well, I think it was already present. But at the same time, you know, in the Church we sometimes have very curious eclipses. I remember, for example, when, just after the war (1945), a Belgian theologian, Father Gilleman, published a book on moral theology, entitled *The Primacy of Charity in Moral Theology* (Westminster, MD: Newman Press, 1959). It was then considered a revolution in moral studies because, for a long time, moral theology contained mainly formal prescriptions. After Gilleman, a very different approach developed that shapes much of our moral theology today. Now, for sincere Christians, the primacy of charity is very obvious.

I think the preferential option for the poor is a very old perspective. We have not just discovered this. What we have done is to take a truth of the Bible and directly relate it to world poverty. If, by hypothesis, it were only an idea discovered in the twentieth century, then the "preferential option for the poor" would not be Christian. We cannot wait twenty centuries to discover such a central point. It is impossible. The notion was present before in different ways. For example, it was present in the founders of many religious congregations. Those founders repeatedly remarked that we need to work with the poor; however, sometimes their followers forgot that vision. The example of Francis of Assisi is very clear, along with that of St. Dominic and many, many others.

Poverty was always a central point in the history of spirituality, and it was always linked to the contemplative life. In the present form, a preferential option for the poor is a central point in the experience and reflection of Latin American Christians. And it seems to me that the Jubilee is a good pre-text (in the sense of something before the text) to remember it, because it is a capital subject of the Jubilee. The poor are first, cries the whole Bible.

Second, the preferential option for the poor is certainly very important for our pastoral work and helps us always keep in mind the universality of the love of God. But it is also very important *in spirituality*. You are all familiar with Henri Nouwen; he is so good in spirituality. Henri was in my country and in Bolivia, twelve or thirteen years ago, and he wrote a beautiful book concerning his trip. The name of Henri's book is *Gracias: Journey in Bolivia and Perú* (San Francisco: Harper & Row, 1983). Henri told me: "For years I was working in spirituality, but seeing the poverty here has convinced me that true Christian spirituality must have a commitment to the poor. For spirituality, the option for the poor is very important."

The preferential option for the poor is also a way of doing theology because it is not the same as reading the Bible from a neutral point of view. In my opinion, the neutral point of view does not exist. A Christian must live his or her life from the perspective of the last ones; it is quite different. Today we see that the preferential option for the poor is central for many biblical scholars and theologians. This option is not only a pastoral issue, but a spiritual and theological one.

My third point was mentioned before. We are really challenged today to find the *face of Jesus Christ in the face of the poor*. You may remember that this idea is present in the document of Puebla and in Santo Domingo too. It was put there by two bishops. We may say this now, almost twenty years after Puebla, because these two bishops are already dead. One was Leonidas Proaño, from Ecuador, an Indian bishop very close to the Ecuadorian Indians. The other one was a

Peruvian, Herman Schmitz, bishop of Lima. Both holy people wrote at Puebla: "We must discover in the faces of the poor in Latin America the face of Jesus Christ." In the insignificant, we must find the significant God in our lives.

It seems to me that this is the meaning of the preferential option for the poor, and I think the preparation for the Jubilee is a very good framework to remember it. I am very surprised in the last few years to discover that the idea of preferential option for the poor, born in some small basic Christian communities in Latin America, is present in the universal church as well as in the magisterium. We were speaking, some minutes before this lecture, of the important letter of the Catholic bishops of this country concerning economic issues (1985). They mentioned the preferential option for the poor as an important criterion to take into consideration. I think we therefore confront a very important point because it is not coming just from theology, it is coming from our Christian revelation. Thank you, my friends.

CHAPTER 3

Forms of Divine Disclosure

DAVID TRACY

INTRODUCTION:
THE FATAL SEPARATIONS OF MODERNITY

A part of our difficulty in addressing the issues of contemporary theology is the failure to consider how the three great separations of modern Western culture have damaged our ability to reflect on modern theology itself.

These three fatal separations are:

first, the separation of feeling and thought;
second, the separation of form and content;
third, the separation of theory and practice.

All three of these peculiarly modern separations are related to one another. Moreover, each is based on an originally helpful distinction that became, in modernity, a separation. Recall, for a moment, the original distinctions and their later modern separations as a part of the larger contemporary attempt to render them again distinctions, not separations.

The modern separations contrast sharply with the relative ease with which either the ancients (see the work of Pierre Hadot) or the medievals (see the work of Jean Le Clerc on the monastic schools and Marie-Dominique Chenu on the scholastics) developed, in their different contexts and schools, valuable distinctions, that they all insisted must not be made into separations, the distinctions of feeling and thought, form and content, practice and theory.

In this lecture, I will not discuss two of these distinctions that have become separations, namely, feeling and thought on the one hand, and theory and practice on the other. In the interests of the time, it seems best in this lecture to concentrate on the one that has received the least attention. For the fact is that, in contemporary theology, the separation of feeling and thought has been the most *healed*, that is, rendered again into a useful distinction, not separation. Consider the many discussions of experience (both personal and communal) as "sources" for contemporary theology. One may note especially how widely accepted now in theology is the practice of the new contextual theologies around the globe; the practice of sustained critical reflection on a people's or culture's experience; the sustained attempts to keep hope alive in the struggle for love and justice; and the solidarity of all Christian communities with the new communities in our now global setting, expressing in both academic and nonacademic forms their important new visions of reality. These new contextual theologies (especially but not solely liberation, political, and feminist-womanist-*mujerista* theologies) do not hesitate to relate, even as they distinguish but never separate, *feeling* and *thought*, *experience* and *reflection*, *witness* and *critique*.

There is, of course, need for further analysis of this first separation, but for the moment allied to the separation of practice and theory, spirituality and theology. The distinction of practice and theory (see the section below)—indeed theory itself as a distinct practice—was a natural distinction (never separation) in all the ancient and medieval schools, including the great Scholastics. This distinction, rendered a separation in the fourteenth-century nominalist crisis and in most of modern neo-Scholasticism, was a distinction again for the great Renaissance humanists (e.g., Erasmus, Colet, Ficino) as well as the great reformers (Luther, Calvin, and their contemporaries).

The third distinction between form and content was crucial in the reflection of all the ancients, even if casually set aside by so many modern theologians and philosophers. As the least reflected upon of the three separations in modern thought, form and content deserves further attention in theology.

FORMS AND FORMS

What, on theological grounds, Hans Urs von Balthasar argued for theology, Louis Dupré argues for philosophy: no interpreter can understand the Western intellectual tradition without focusing on the phenomenon of form, from its beginning to its present crisis, which can now be seen as a crisis of form. Indeed, the central ideal of Western thought from its beginning in Greece (or even, before classical Greece, as argued by Mircea Eliade in his studies of archaic religious manifestations) was the idea of the real as, in essence, its appearance in form. Dupré interprets this centrality of form (the principal leitmotif of his study of modernity) so that form grounds the ancient and medieval onto-theological synthesis. For the ancients, the essence of the real and our knowledge of it consists ultimately of form. Form, moreover, shows forth the real in harmonious appearance: whether in sensuous image as in Greek sculpture; in mathematics as in Pythagoras; in the forms of tragedy which render some aesthetic harmony even to chaos and strife; above all, through the ancient philosophical turn to reflective form in the soul or mind. The real appears in an orderly way and thus becomes (even in tragedy) harmonious appearance. This aesthetic, that is, form-focused understanding of the real, provided the ultimate grounding for any harmonious synthesis of the cosmic, of the divine and the human realms among the ancients. A harmonious synthesis is a difficult thought to comprehend for us late-twentieth-century heirs of the fragmentation of all syntheses. It is even more difficult for us as inheritors of a hermeneutics of suspicion, which suggests that every form may merely mask indeterminacy and every appearance or manifestation may always already hide a strife involving both disclosure and concealment.

Nevertheless, both critics and proponents of classical, medieval and much modern thought (Bruno to Hegel) cannot grasp Western thought without dwelling on the centrality of form. For the premoderns, what appears or manifests itself through form is not our subjective construction but the very showing forth, through form, of the real. For the Greeks, real being begins with intelligible form, that is, with a multiplicity, chaos, strife rendered somehow orderly and harmonious through form. The Jewish and Christian thinkers accepted the centrality of form but could not accept the necessity of form in Greek and Roman thought. The Greek gods need the form principle; indeed, the form is divine and the divine is form for the Greeks. For the Jew, Christian, and Muslim, God creates form. But as long as God is not understood as exclusively a purely transcendent will, and as long as God's actions are not read exclusively through efficient causality, then form survives, indeed, prevails: now through the Creator-God's formal, immanent causality. For Christian thought, moreover, the doctrine of the Word grounded this reality of form in the central Christian doctrines of Christology and Trinity.

This principle of reality manifested *as real* in and through harmonious form "in-form-ed" the Western philosophical onto-theological tradition from Plato through Hegel. For Plato, with all his constant rethinking of *form*, especially in *Parmenides*, form resided in some manner within the appearing objects of which it constituted the intelligible essence. As the determining factor of that intelligibility (and thereby reality), form also surpassed the objects. In all Greek philosophy (including Aristotle, despite his critique of Plato on form), being is defined in terms of form. Moreover, form's dependence is to be understood primarily, though not exclusively, in terms of participation. The same is also true, it might be added, of archaic and Greek religion described as manifestation (Eliade) or, as Hegel nicely named Greek religion, the religion of beauty. The same centrality of form, as Balthasar brilliantly shows, is true of any form of Christianity faithful to the incarnational principle and to a properly theological understanding of Word as Logos, that is, a manifestation in and through form. Indeed, even for Hegel, all content attains its truth in and through form.

In my judgment, we can render this new interest in form explicitly hermeneutical in philosophy and theology. Hermeneutics, after all, since the revisions of Heidegger by first Gadamer and then Ricoeur, has articulated a position on truth very like that implicit in much contemporary discussion. The ancients hold that truth does mean *to be justified* (as for the moderns), but that justification can be found principally in the sense that truth means participation in being (not construction of it) as manifested through form. This ancient sense is also the one argued by modern hermeneutics: first, by Hans-Georg Gadamer in his insistence in *Truth and Method* that truth is fundamentally disclosure, and is best rendered through form (*Dar-stellung*, not *Vor-stellung*); and second, and most carefully, by Paul Ricoeur in his contemporary argument that truth is primordially manifestation, and only derivatively correspondence or even coherence. Truth as manifestation is allied to Ricoeur's further hermeneutical question of how the world of the possibility of the manifestation is rendered through the forms of composition, genre, and style. Any philosopher who argues, on contemporary grounds, in favor of a hermeneutical understanding of truth as primordially manifestation through some form (as I also have in other writing) cannot but be heartened by the new emphasis on centrality of form in contemporary philosophy and theology.

THE TURN TO THE OTHER AND TO OTHER FORMS IN CHRISTIAN THEOLOGY

The turn to the other takes many forms in postmodernity. Every form is an interruption of the role of the same, more often understood as the reign of the modern. Interruption itself, takes many forms. Sometimes it comes as sheer interruptive event, power, gift. At other times it comes as revelation and grace. Where transgression often serves as a first sign of a postmodern arrival, the reality of gift and its economy is often a second and more explicitly theological sign of the presence of postmodernity. As with the earlier dialectical theologians (especially Karl Barth), both event language and revelation language have returned, if for very different reasons, to theology. Both languages now return not so much to retrieve some aspect of premodernity (although that too becomes a real possibility), but rather to disrupt or interrupt the continuities and similarities masking the increasingly deadening sameness of the modern worldview. *Event* is that which cannot be accounted for in the present order but disrupts it by happening. *Gift* transgresses the present economy and calls it into question. *Revelation* is the event-gift of the Other's self-manifestation.

Revelation disrupts the continuities, the similarities, and the communalities of modern *religion*.

Many forms of philosophy and theology partake of such otherness. With the fine exception of that form of analytical philosophy naming itself *Christian philosophy* (and thereby, considering *revelation*, not only *religion*), much philosophy of religion seems capable only of further scholasticism or of the relatively untroubled, not to say relaxed, postmodernity of Richard Rorty. Moreover, most forms of *philosophy of religion* (a discipline invented in and for modernity) are far too caught in their own disciplinary modernism to even consider the otherness of revelation as worthy of their attention. On the other hand, all those forms of philosophy in which *otherness* and *difference* have become central categories now find modernity more a problematic concept, and less a ready solution. These philosophies of otherness and difference have become, in fact if not in name, postmodern. Often this occurs through a self-conscious recovery of the non-Enlightenment, even at times the non-Greek, resources of Western culture itself: witness Emmanuel Levinas's brilliant recovery of ethics as first philosophy, partly made possible by his recovery of the Judaic strands of our culture; witness Pierre Hadot's and Martha Nussbaum's distinct recoveries of the pluralistic, literary (Nussbaum), and spiritual exercises (Hadot) aspects of pluralistic Hellenistic rather than only classic Hellenic culture; witness Jean-Luc Marion's brilliant recovery of pseudo-Dionysius or Julia Kristeva's recovery of the love mystics; witness Jacques Derrida's interest in (and critique of) the traditions of apophatic theology; and witness John Caputo's recent Judeo-Christian philosophical critique of Heidegger's obsession with the Greeks.

The list of genuinely postmodern philosophical exercises could easily be expanded. Some of these exercises (as, curiously, with the ancients) make it difficult to distinguish a philosophical from a theological position any longer: recall the work of Mark C. Taylor, Robert Scharlemann or Edith Wyschogrod. Others, especially in French philosophy, speak their descriptions of the other in more familiar theological terms: the gift is explicitly named *grace*; the *event* of the Other is named the *revelation* event of the Other's self-manifestation. Indeed, those new postmodern theological options have exploded in a hundred new cultural and theological forms.

Surely the very question of form itself is what should most command our attention. My own belief is that occurring across the Christian theological spectrum is an event of major import: the attempt to free Christian theology from the now smothering embrace of modernity, an event which is as difficult, as conflictual, and as painful as the earlier (equally necessary) attempt in early modernity to free theology from the suffocating embrace of premodern modes of thought. In every discipline, including theology, some moderns have now become the most defensive and troubled thinkers of all. They always seem to be searching for one more round of the premodern versus modern debate in order to display their honest modern scruples and arguments one more time. Fortunately for them, there are more than enough fundamentalist groups (that curious *underside* of the modern dilemma) to allow the *modern* debate to continue.

Unfortunately for the moderns, however, the more serious debate, I believe, has shifted to one they continue to avoid: the debate on the *unthought* aspects of modernity itself. Was the modern turn to the subject also a turn to the same? Was the *religionizing* of all theology more of that same? Is the modern form of argument adequate to understand genuine otherness and difference? Is not modern liberal thought far more engendered, colonialist, at times even racist, classist, and above all Eurocentric, than it seems capable of acknowledging? These questions begin to haunt the modern conscience like a guilty romance. For some philosophers and theologians the only honest option is to find better ways to honor otherness and difference by transgressing the modern liberal pieties when it is necessary in order to honor in thought as in life the otherness manifested in Jesus Christ and the otherness explosively disclosed in all the many new theologies of our day.

The question of form itself, I repeat, is one way to begin to address these new theological questions with new resources for thought and action. Christian theology should never be form-less, even in its most apophatic, that is, form-less moments (for example, Meister Eckhart). Christian theology should always be determined in its understanding of God and humanity by its belief in the form-of-forms, the divine-human form, Jesus Christ, that form which must inform all Christian understanding of God and transform all Christian understanding of human possibility for thought and, above all, action.

There is no serious form of *Christian* theology which is not Christomorphic. This is a more accurate designation of the christological issue, I believe, than the more familiar but confusing word *Christo-centric*. For theology is not Christocentric but theocentric, although it is so only by means of its Christomorphism. But my present concern is what form this Christomorphism might take in the present situation of the turn to the other. The answer, I believe, is ready at hand in all the new theologies occurring across the whole Christian world (not only in its Euro-American corner). The answer is likely to occur in even more diverse cultural forms in the future. The answer, whether evangelical or mystical, whether Euro-American or African, whether feminist or womanist, or *mujerista*, whether explicitly postmodern or only implicitly so, is the explosion of what Gustavo Gutiérrez and others have named the mystical-political form which contemporary theology needs to take.

My own suggestion is that this now familiar mystical-political naming, although resonant to many of the needs of our moment, is not the most adequate way to describe the fuller range of options for rendering the Other in new forms. To render the Other in new forms, we may consider the following hypothesis of the fuller spectrum of possible forms needed (and, as it happens, available) for our present question of postmodern theology's turn to the other.

Any Christian theology which claims its basic continuity with its biblical roots (as, I believe, Christian theology must if it is seriously Christian) may find what it needs in the full spectrum of forms in the Bible itself. The two most basic religious forms in the Bible are the prophetic and the meditative (wisdom) forms. From these two forms and their dialectic emerge the fuller spectrum of past, present, and likely future forms of Christian theology.

First, the prophetic. The prophet speaks not because he or she wishes to, but because God as Other demands it. The prophet speaks on behalf of the other—the neighbor, especially the poor, the oppressed, and marginal other. Jesus is the Jewish eschatological prophet bespeaking the Other for the sake of all others. There is no way around the prophetic core of Christian self-understanding. Even our earliest Christologies in Mark and Paul come in prophetic form. Not only the liberation and evangelical theologies but all serious Christian theology must maintain that prophetic form or admit that its transformation into some reality has become something perhaps rich and strange but no longer Christian, that is, prophetic.

That prophetic core, in turn, can move in two directions. First, the prophetic insight can be taken in a generalizing direction wherein its religious or revelatory core is seen, at its heart, also as ethics. This is what Emmanuel Levinas has found in his simultaneous discovery that ethics is first philosophy and that true ethics is grounded in the face of the other. The other, the biblical neighbor, is what no ontological totality can ever control. The temptation to totalizing modes of thought is disrupted once and for all by the glimpse of the Infinite in the face of the other and the Infinite's (or the Other's) ethical command *Do not kill me.* Is it really so surprising that Levinas's work has become so central not only for Jewish thought but also for Christian liberation theology (see Dussel) with its instinctive prophetic-ethical sense for the other, especially the preferred other of the prophets, the poor, the marginal, and the oppressed.

One or another version of this prophetic form determines the new kind of Christian theological ethics in many postmodern political, feminist, womanist, and liberation theologies across the Christian world. The difference between a postmodern ethics focused on the Other and others on the one hand, and the kinds of ethical positions developed in modern liberal theologies focused on the modern autonomous self and its rational obligations on the other, is clear. Some move to ethics (or with the ancients, more accurately the ethical-political realm) is necessary for Christian theology. Postmodern positions (like Levinas's) seem to me far more hermeneutically faithful to a prophetic self-understanding than the more familiar modern deontological and teleological Christian ethical options.

But the prophetic center can also break away from any generalizing move at all in favor of the intensification, indeed transgression, of the prophetic form into a radically disruptive apocalyptic form. *When prophesy fails, apocalyptic takes over.* And so it may. History then becomes interpreted not as continuity at all but as radical interruption. In philosophy, the apocalyptic urgency of the early Frankfurt thinkers (especially Benjamin and Adorno) will return as it surely does in Johann Baptist Metz's apocalyptic political theology. His theology yields great ethical-political urgency, which is driven by the reality of the memory of suffering in the passion narratives and the narratives of all suffering peoples, but also does not yield generalizing ethical principles. In our more American theological culture, this is especially the case in African-American and Hispanic theologies and their amazing return to the narrations of their peoples and the theological sophistication of the songs, the spirituals and blues of African-American culture, the chants of laments and outbursts of joy in Hispanic cultures. When apocalypse is understood in and through the forms of excess, transgression, and negation of continuity, then apocalyptic returns as the favored form of many radicalized political theologies.

In the meantime, the other great biblical form, the meditative or wisdom form, may also move in these same two directions. First, its center: the meditative form turns away from the more historical and ethical prophetic core of the Bible in order to reflect upon our relationships to the cosmos and to face the kind of limit-situations (death, guilt, anxiety, despair, joy, peace, hope) which human beings as human beings will always experience. Job and Lamentations will always speak their meditative, penetrating truth to anyone capable of facing the tragedy which is at the heart of every human existence. The Gospel of John—that meditative rendering of the common Christian narrative—will always describe the beauty and glory of the whole of reality (even the cross as lifting up and disclosure of Glory in John!) to all those capable of genuine meditation on the limit-experiences of peace, joy, beauty, and love. Meditative humans, then as now, will turn to intelligence and love, to nature and to cosmos, to mind and to body, to aid their reflections on the vision of life and the wisdom disclosed by the biblical narratives for our common human limit-experiences.

When these meditative positions make even further generalizing moves they are more likely to develop profound participatory metaphysics (like Platonism in all its splendid forms). When more ethically oriented, a wisdom ethics will prove an aesthetic ethics of appreciation of the good and of beauty (like Whitehead and Hartshorne). When more historically conscious, these meditative positions will develop into a hermeneutical philosophy disclosing the dialogical character of all reality. A wisdom-grounded metaphysics (never totalizing if hermeneutically faithful to its biblical core) and an aesthetics will unite to relate themselves to some form of prophetic ethics, more likely in these traditions an ethics of the Good.

However, the meditative traditions need not stay in those participatory moments. They too may also take their own turn to the other. Then the meditation is intensified to the point of becoming transgressive of all participation, as typically with postmodern recoveries of the more radical mystical traditions as when even meditative forms become fragments. Love then becomes not relationality or overflow but sheer excess and transgression, from Bataille through Kristeva. Radically apophatic Christian mysticism (for example, Meister Eckhart) becomes a genuine option for contemporary thought. The recovery of mystical readings of the prophetic core of Judaism and Christianity is one of the surest signs of a postmodern sensibility. In a similar fashion the return of the repressed *pagan* emphasis on nature becomes an equally clear sign, as Scholem insisted, of the presence of a new mystical reading of a prophetic tradition.

This fuller spectrum of a seemingly endless series of new prophetic and meditative forms in the new theologies across the globe will surely increase. As both cross-cultural sensibilities and interreligious dialogue take further hold on serious Christian theology, moreover, this prophetic-meditative spectrum will increase yet again. Theology will never again be tameable by any totality system—any system—modern or premodern or postmodern. For theology does not bespeak a totality. Christian theology, at its best, is the voice of the Other through all those others who have tasted, prophetically and meditatively, the Infinity disclosed in the kenotic reality of Jesus Christ.

CHAPTER 4

Memoirs and Meaning

JILL KER CONWAY

I t is a great honor and pleasure to participate in this historic award. When the invitation came I realized how grateful I was to be asked to reflect on the way my Catholic faith had affected my scholarly life. I had never before given the question the sustained attention it clearly warranted. So I am in your debt for an important stimulus to reflection.

My Christian faith has certainly led me to my interest in the moral and spiritual dimensions of the journey in time we all make, and since my intellectual bent is literary, I have focused my attention on the way we narrate life histories, and the forms and conventions which define what can be thought and said about those travels.

But when I speak about my Christian faith I must make clear that mine was not a typical encounter with Christian institutions as a child and adolescent. My introducer mentioned that I grew up in a very remote part of rural Australia. My parents' sheep station was about five hundred miles west of Sydney; the population density of the region was about one in twenty square miles. The annual rainfall was less than ten inches of rain a year making it semi-arid desert country. Our closest town was forty miles away, and there was no Catholic church closer than one hundred miles. So, as a child, I did not encounter institutional religion.

The time of my birth increased this isolation because I was five years old when the 1939–45 war broke out. Most able-bodied men in rural Australia then joined the armed services; my two older brothers were then in boarding school, and so I worked beside my father on the ranch rather than doing correspondence school with a governess. My mother had concluded correctly that since I could read I could teach myself what was necessary one afternoon a week, and I was a farm worker on the other six and a half days.

Much of that time was spent alone herding sheep and cattle, a solitary life, almost an Old Testament existence. It never surprised me that the Old Testament prophets were alone when God spoke to them. How else could it be? For a child whose days were solitary without the sound of another human voice, not even the sound of songbirds, nothing but the wind and the desert, most of the time was spent thinking about the relationship of human beings to nature.

And the question kept being reinforced because of encounters with Tribal Aboriginals, hunter-gatherers whose culture was many thousands of years old. Those made one ask: what are we white people doing here? More existentially pressing was: why am I here? and what am I supposed to be doing? These questions don't arise so early for children in a man-made environment. There are people all around like oneself, and the built environment seems to have been made for you. But the long silent days and the contemplation of nature made me ask the theological questions which are the grounding of a religious sensibility long before I had ever seen a church.

Events also produced a powerful interest in questions of free will and determinism. The arrival of drought and other natural disasters prompted me to question the efficacy of human will, and to see human beings as tiny entities in face of the vastness and impersonality of nature.

Those two powerful interests shaped how I read and what I thought about. There was no Sunday worship, just the Bible to read, and a father who was a devout Catholic, ready to talk about the creation and his understanding of God. Since these discussions took place in the absence of any institutional church or liturgy, there was nothing to object to, no exercise of clerical authority about which to be outraged. I knew only the questions and the vastness of the universe. There was no sacramental life, a discovery made much later when we moved to the city.

When I did encounter institutional religion at boarding school and in college it was initially at the margin rather than in the center of my attention, because I already had my questions and was intent on finding the answers my own way. And that way was through the study of history. Like all young undergraduates who read classical philosophy I was fascinated by the Greek world, its educational ideals, and its notion of *arête*, the pure excellence of form which could be mental or physical or both. And the notion that all actions or processes had an end toward which they moved, whether by natural processes or by artifice, fitted with my quest for order and an understanding of causation in the universe. It remained only to encounter St. Augustine to see these concepts transformed into an inner spiritual quest for a relationship to God, to set me studying the history of the Roman and Byzantine Church and the great religious communities of the medieval world.

These concepts and the systems of thought within which they operated were focused upon the male experience, so it was natural for me to seek, through my own intellectual life, a way of relating them to a female experience. In my case this quest was not shaped by rejection of a male hierarchy, but rather in a Greek manner to arrive at a whole rather than a partial view of things.

So, I began my career as a research historian studying the lives of women. What was their *arête*? What was their relation to God? What combination of nature and art produced the *telos* of a female life? To what did God call them, not as defined by men, but as lived in their experience?

At Harvard I chose as a dissertation topic a collective biography of the first generation of American women to undertake graduate education; women seeking to create knowledge rather than receiving it from others. They were born around 1860 and died in the 1930s. They were the founders of the female professions—social work, nursing, librarianship, elementary and secondary school teaching. All were powerful social reformers who played a major part in shaping the social and political thought of the Progressive era. They mostly studied in Europe, because in their generation, only Cornell, via Sage College, encouraged women to undertake graduate study fields such as economics and social theory. Collectively they believed that their education had given them a calling to develop a larger theory of democratic institutions which included women as full citizens, and, because mostly the learned professions were not open to them, they put their ideas into action as social reformers.

Many of their names will be familiar to you. M. Carey Thomas (1857–1935), founder of Bryn Mawr; Jane Addams (1860–1935), founder of Hull House and the profession of social work; Florence Kelley(1859–1932), first translator of Marx and Engels in the United States, founder of the Consumers' League, and dynamic activist for the elimination of child labor and for improved working conditions for industrial workers; Alice Hamilton(1869–1970), founder of the field of industrial medicine. All of them knew one another, all kept diaries, and all corresponded with one another.[1]

I found them absolutely riveting as subjects of research. They were ambitious to do great things, and openly so. They talked to one another about creating a new kind of democratic society shaped by the life experience of women citizens as well as men. And they felt called to do so—called by history, by the fact of their access to education, and by their understanding of a divinity they did not think of in male terms. They were struggling to understand being female in the context of the Civil War and its aftermath, and in a rapidly industrializing society.

They were certainly not controlled by contemporary notions of female propriety. They were interested in and active in politics when this was thought unfeminine, always ready to take the train to Washington to find their way around Capitol Hill and work tirelessly as lobbyists. They didn't worry about not being able to vote because they took the abolition movement as their model. They knew how to organize, and they were *very* effective.

Because they left ample archives of personal and professional documents, I came to know them well, perhaps better than any of their contemporaries, and possibly better than they knew themselves. You see a life in the round when you can read diaries, personal letters, the comments of their critics, the assessments of friends and enemies, press clippings, and how ensuing generations responded to them.

What I liked about them was their courage, their intellectual drive, and their completely instrumental view of themselves and their public roles. For instance, when they launched what was to be a successful campaign to outlaw child labor, their discussion of the respective roles they would play was totally pragmatic. It could be paraphrased like this, "Who looks best in press photographs? Florence Kelley looks best in press photographs. She should announce the campaign. Who is the best lobbyist? Jane Addams. She should go to Washington. Who is the best fundraiser to support the public relations campaign? We'll put her to work at once." Clearly they enjoyed fighting for a cause, and were strategic in their assessment of what reforms could be successfully won. Their celebrations when they won were very high-spirited because they knew they had laid the groundwork, chosen the moment, and deployed their talents correctly.

Naturally, I looked forward to reading the memoirs and diaries of these skilled politicians. But I was disappointed. When it came to telling their life stories they suppressed all of the ambition, all of the savvy interest in power and politics, all the joy in battle. They told their stories as though they were the sweetest, gentlest maiden ladies one could meet. They concealed the reasons for their success, and presented themselves as people to whom causes happen, rather than as the strong leaders they were.

What was even more troubling was that they didn't acknowledge thinking and planning for their actions, but, rather, made them seem emotional and intuitive. When Jane Addams founded Hull House, the pioneer social settlement that became the model for American reform communities, she did so after years of study in Europe. She wanted to found a community for educated American women, so in the process of thinking about it she visited Ursuline and Benedictine convents, utopian socialist communities outside Paris, and Toynbee Hall in South London, a major British reform community aimed at helping London's poor. These were all aids to her in thinking about how she could found a community in Chicago's slums, where educated women could be interpreters of America and American values to immigrants, and interpreters of the immigrant laboring population to native-born Americans. She felt called to try to prevent class divisions appearing in the United States, a calling that came from her loyalty to her family's devotion to the memory of Lincoln and the abolition of slavery. During her years in Europe she also became widely read in British and European social thought, and had a cosmopolitan understanding of the social consequences of industrialization.

But, when she wrote her autobiography she didn't mention the years of study and the intellectual roots of her actions. She wrote:

> It is hard to tell just when the very simple plan which afterward developed into the Settlement first began to form itself in my mind. It may have been even before I went to Europe for the second time, but I gradually became convinced that it would be a good thing to rent a house in a part of the city where many primitive and actual needs are found, in which young women who had been given over too exclusively to study, might restore a balance of activity along traditional lines and learn of life from life itself.[2]

What is remarkable about this statement is that it implies that she had little conscious thought on the subject (the thought *formed itself*) and that she will not report a specific time when she took a decision to act as an outcome of her systematic thought on the problem of poverty. So the interesting question is—why did she distance herself as far as possible from being an actor in her own story?

And she is not alone. My study of women's autobiography shows that this distancing is the norm. Here is another example. Margaret Sanger was the determined sexual radical who led the birth control movement in the United States. Sanger's mother had had fourteen pregnancies, and Sanger was convinced that her mother's early death from tuberculosis was brought on by the repeated births. She vowed as a young woman to do something to prevent such deaths in the future. She trained as a nurse and began her career in New York City, developing an obstetrics practice in the Lower East Side of Manhattan. She wanted to collect case records to demonstrate how repeated pregnancies and poor nutrition damaged the health of immigrant women. In order to build her practice she had flyers printed that read *Margaret A. Sanger, Obstetrics Nurse, Available for Deliveries.* These were posted around the Lower East Side and consequently she began to receive calls to attend deliveries there. But in her autobiography she writes, "I did not really like working in the Lower East Side. Poverty was not attractive, but more and more my calls began to come from the Lower East Side of Manhattan as though I were being pulled there by a destiny beyond my control." (Margaret Sanger, *An Autobiography*, 1938). Here again the speaker is distancing herself from the action she herself has brought about.

This style of narrative is in sharp contrast to the standard male narrative, in which planning, action, and agency are the main themes. Let those who doubt this assertion read James Watson on the discovery of DNA or Lee Iacocca on the rescue of the Chrysler Corporation, or Henry Ford's narrative of the founding of the Ford Motor Company.[3] Ambition is proudly acknowledged in these narratives, planning is placed front and center of the story, and the narrator clearly is the agent of what happens. This striking difference, which has deep historical roots, has been of interest to me as a teacher of history, as a writer and student of the genre of autobiography, and as someone with a deep concern for the moral development of women.

As a teacher of young people in transition from late adolescence to young adulthood, it has bothered me that when I counsel a young man about his life choices and his quest for a vocation, I can pull down from my bookshelves any number of male narratives which describe how the author found his calling and pursued it. But if I am counseling a young woman the task is more difficult because even the greatest women leaders appear to need to conceal the springs of their actions, and to attribute what motivates them to fate, destiny, anything but their own moral growth and development.

This concealment seems a serious problem to me because the years between eighteen and twenty-two are the years when young people are most open to moral questions about the use of the talents they possess. Or, to put it in Greek terms, young persons are open to searching for the telos of the life they have been given. But how are young women to hear the call if women tell their life stories in ways that obscure the unfolding of a vocation?

I think Freud was correct when he said that love and work were the two deepest structures of the human personality, so a tradition of female self-narrative which discourages acknowledging the quest for the work that harnesses our talents most creatively, makes the transition to young adulthood more difficult and stressful for young women than it is for their male counterparts. And, quite correctly, the Catholic notion of the formation of a religious sensibility stresses prayerful examination of one's vocation as one of the major tasks of a young life. This is difficult to do if cultural tradition requires distancing oneself from agency in this task.

Because, as we can see from Addams and Sanger, the relation of self to agency has been difficult for women, autobiography is a literary genre which illuminates the ways this difficulty is experienced, or, put another way, how gender categories shape our consciousness.

Besides this specific gender concern many universal questions are raised by autobiographical writing. How does one construct a narrative in which the narrator is both subject and object? How does one as reader disentangle the person speaking from the cultural categories in which she or he has been taught to organize memory? When and how do those generally accepted life plots change? Think, for example, of the standard plot of grand opera which decrees that the heroine must die in the last act. The soprano meets the tenor in act 1. They fall in love and are parted in the second act. And shortly after they are reunited in the third act, she dies of tuberculosis, or she commits suicide, or she is poisoned, or she is murdered. This is a plot that says the woman's story ends when she meets the tenor, a plot convention that continued in the modern novel. Female authors would bring their narratives to an end by saying "And so reader, I married him." Or, like Hemingway's heroine in *A Farewell to Arms,* the author has the heroine die in childbirth in the last chapter, a plot convention that says that a woman's life story ends when she meets the hero.

Fortunately those forms are being changed by modern feminism, and by the many aspects of modern mass society that make it increasingly difficult to narrate a male life as a heroic odyssey. So, from the Civil War onward stories of warfare show us the warrior as victim, a theme strengthened by the experience of 1914–18, and given new force by the ambiguities of conflict against popular insurgencies such as Vietnam.

It is those changes which I believe have led to a growing readership for autobiography, and a growing interest in the genre by literary scholars. The expanding readership comes about because it is impossible to write a memoir, even the worst ghostwritten variety, without tackling many great humanistic themes. Is there free will? What are the sources of moral strength or weakness? Where do our motives come from? How are they shaped by others? How does a person find her or his vocation? In what language and through what processes in the psyche does God speak to us?

And literary scholars have become more interested in narratives where subject and object overlap, and the narrator knows, as no one else can, how an event was experienced. Georges Gusdorf, one of the scholars who first focused attention on autobiography in the 1950s, spoke about the writing of one's own life narrative as "the knowing of knowing." He also called such narratives "scriptures of the self" comparing them to the narratives of Old Testament prophets whose examination of their lives was undertaken to give witness to a relationship to God.[4]

We have no greater example of this than the book of Job:

Let me have silence, and I will speak, and let come on me what may. I will take my flesh in my teeth, and put my life in my hands. Behold, he will slay me; I have no hope; yet I will defend my ways to his face. . . . Listen carefully to my words, and let my declaration be in your ears. Behold, I have prepared my case; I know that I shall be vindicated. Who is there that will contend with me? For then I would be silent and die. Only grant two things to me. Then I will not hide myself from thy Face. . . . Then call, and I will answer; or let me speak, and do thou reply to me.[5]

Today, most people don't read the Bible, but they are still hungry for meaning, for any narrative that tries to draw out the meaning of a life. I think this is why there is an intense interest today in personal narratives, and why those that ring psychologically, emotionally, and historically true attract a wide readership. For that reason one might think of the writing of memoir as a religious act, an honest attempt to share experience with others, and to involve self and reader in drawing meaning from experience.

If we see the central fact of a Christian experience as the journey in time toward an encounter with God, then memory is our most profoundly spiritual faculty. In my most recent book I've tried to spell out its importance even for nonbelievers.

> Until we lose it we take memory for granted. Along with language it is the force that makes us human. It gives us the cultural context for the miraculous power of communication. Memory was Mnemosyne for the Greeks and Minerva with her owl for the Romans—a powerful goddess with a beneficent face. We need to cultivate her, because it matters how we remember things.
>
> If we remember the past as a series of chaotic events governed by an impersonal and nonmoral fate or luck, we create a similar kind of future in our mind's eye, and that prophecy is usually self-fulfilling. If we see the past as fully determined—by economic forces, by genetic codes, even by birth order and relationship to parents—we see ourselves as victims of those forces, with our best hope a kind of stoic resignation. If we see our past as a moral and spiritual journey in time, our imagined future will continue that quest. We might not use the imagery of Dame Julian of Norwich, but we will be in the same existential position that she was, pondering the intersection of our tiny point of human consciousness with the metaphysical pattern she called the mind of God.
>
> We travel through life guided by an inner life plot—part the creation of family, part the internalization of broader social norms, part the function of our imaginations and our own capacity for insight into ourselves, part from our groping to understand the universe in which the planet we inhabit is a speck. When we speak about our memories we do so through literary forms that seem to capture the universals of human experience—the quest, the romance, the odyssey, the tragic or the comic mode. Yet we are all unique and so are our stories. We should pay close attention to our stories. Polish their imagery. Find their positive rather than their negative form. Search for the ways we experience life

differently from the inherited version and edit the plot accordingly, keeping our eyes on the philosophical implications of the changes we make. Was this action free? Was that one determined? How does the intersection of the two change the trajectory of a life?[6]

CHAPTER 5

Catholic and Intellectual:
Conjunction or Disjunction?

MARCIA L. COLISH

My title, "Catholic and Intellectual: Conjunction or Disjunction?" directs attention to the copula, "and." Does this word bind "Catholic" and "intellectual" in a harmonious and mutually supportive union? Or, does it place these terms in an either/or, contrasting, or even confrontational stance? To be sure, some non-Catholics opt for the second interpretation. As they see it, if one is a Catholic one has to cash in one's brains. In particular, if one is a Catholic theologian, one is constrained to play Charlie McCarthy to the Edgar Bergen of whoever occupies the throne of Peter, or his self-appointed scriptwriter. Oddly enough, this same attitude can also be found in some Catholic circles, on the part of some would-be ventriloquists and those they have managed to convince. Proponents of this view also seek to obfuscate the distinction between the creeds of the church and the handful of infallible papal rulings made since 1870 and the large number of other doctrines which Catholic theologians may legitimately debate and on which they, and the rest of the faithful, may hold their own positions.

How should Catholic academics who want to dissociate themselves from intraconfessional anti-intellectualism go about it? In reflecting on these matters, it occurred to me that my own academic specialty, medieval intellectual history, provides some valuable insights and rationales. At the same time, it occurred to me that it would be worth considering how more recent thinkers had addressed this, and related, themes. So I decided to consult two previous commentators

on the university, and the church-related university, John Henry Newman and Jaroslav Pelikan. Newman published *The Idea of a University*
in 1855 and Pelikan published his reflections on that book, *The Idea of
a University: A Reexamination*, in 1992. Although separated by the At-
lantic and by almost 150 years, these authors, I found, had much to
say of interest on this topic and to this audience, and much that I
could use as the springboard for my own reflections on the subject.

First, Newman. Particular historical circumstances inspired him to
write *The Idea of a University*. In the 1850s, in England, one had to be
a communicant of the Anglican Church in order to study and teach
at a university. Indeed, Newman's conversion to Catholicism forced
him to resign his fellowship at Oriel College, Oxford. In response to
this situation, which effectively barred non-Anglicans from the learned
professions unless they had studied abroad, the decision was made by
the Irish hierarchy to found a Catholic university in that part of the
British Isles. Newman served as its first rector. It was in connection
with this assignment that he outlined what we would call today the
"mission statement" of the Irish Catholic University, in the lectures
and occasional pieces published as *The Idea of a University*. In short,
rather than projecting a Platonic ideal of a university, Newman aimed
at explaining the policies he actually intended to implement in this
newly launched institution.

There are a number of key themes Newman emphasizes in de-
scribing the educational objectives of the new university, many of
which still merit our consideration. The Irish Catholic university, he
notes, teaches the liberal arts and also has faculties for specialized postgraduate study in the sciences, medicine, and law, equipping degree
recipients to enter the learned professions. The university teaches theology as well, not only as a postgraduate discipline but also as a branch
of liberal studies. Newman stresses the idea that theology should be
taught as a university discipline; he does not want to see it ghettoized
in seminaries or monasteries, aimed exclusively at the vocational formation of clergy-in-training. In this connection, Newman looks back
to theology as a university discipline in medieval scholasticism, while
at the same time he anticipates religious studies as a branch of the
humanities, themes to which I will return.

While he certainly pays attention to the learned disciplines that lead to professional accreditation, Newman's primary concern is the BA curriculum, the liberal arts, and the qualities of mind they should impart whether or not students go on to postgraduate work. In the academic jargon of today, Newman is interested in "outcomes assessment," that is, what undergraduates actually retain after commencement day. His term for this is Liberal Knowledge. Liberal Knowledge, as Newman defines it, has two critical aspects. First, it produces the habits of mind and modes of behavior that characterize the gentleman—a term both gender-specific and class-specific in Newman's historical context. If we want to subscribe to this notion we will also certainly want to qualify Newman's concept, making it more inclusive. Second, desirable as these attainments may be, Newman argues that intellectual virtue should not be confused with moral virtue. To be sure, intellectual virtue can, and should, be put to the service of moral ends. But, in and of itself, it is morally neutral. It may also be put to the service of greed, destructiveness, and the *libido dominandi*. By itself, intellectual virtue does not add one jot or title to the moral stature of its possessor. Nor is it proof against the passions and sinful impulses that incline fallen humanity to folly and vice.

For Newman, then, a church-related university is not, automatically, a school for virtue. Nor should it be envisioned as such. I'd like to read a fairly lengthy quotation from *The Idea of a University* in which Newman lays this point on the line:

> Knowledge is one thing, virtue is another; good sense is not conscience, refinement is not humility, nor is largeness and justice of view faith. Philosophy, however enlightened, however profound, gives no command over the passions, no influential motives, no vivifying principles. . . . It is well to have a cultivated intellect, a delicate taste, a candid, equitable, dispassionate mind, a noble and courteous bearing in the conduct of life; these are the connatural qualities of a large knowledge; they are the objects of a University; . . . but . . . they are no guarantee for sanctity or even for conscientiousness. . . . Their admirers persist in arrogating for them a praise to which they have no claim. Quarry the granite

rock with razors, or moor the vessel with a thread of silk; then may you hope with such keen and delicate instruments as human knowledge and reason to contend against those giants, the passions and the pride of man. . . . To open the mind, to correct it, to refine it, to enable it to know, to digest, master, rule, and use the knowledge, to give it power over its own faculties, application, flexibility, method, and critical exactness, sagacity, resource, address, eloquent expression, is an object as intelligible as the cultivation of virtue, while, at the same time, it is absolutely distinct from it.[1]

While agreeing that Liberal Knowledge can serve morality and religion, then, Newman also notes that it can be used by scoffers and critics of morality and religion. With respect to the Christian tradition, he concludes, Liberal Knowledge "proves, in the event, sometimes its serviceable ally, sometimes . . . an insidious and dangerous foe."[2]

Having thus crisply dissociated himself from the ancient Greek philosophical maxim "To virtue, knowledge," Newman turns to another of his central concerns, what he calls the duties of the church toward knowledge, in a church-related university. In this connection, his prescriptions have a strikingly modern look and are fully applicable today. Newman begins by observing that all the arts and sciences, be they secular or theological, have their own proper methods and criteria, their own scope and legitimacy in their own spheres. He is vigorously opposed to reductionism of any kind, from whatever quarter. Practitioners in all fields, he argues, must recognize, and respect, the norms and procedures followed in other fields. It follows, from this principle, that the university does not delimit or censor what is studied or what books are to be read. It is interesting to note, here, that Newman sees the greatest challenge to Christianity as coming from the arts and humanities, not from the natural sciences. In digesting that fact, it is worth keeping in mind that Newman wrote before the Darwinian revolution. And, he is a throwback to the view that Aristotle is the "master of those who know" in the sciences, Galileo, Newton, and others to the contrary notwithstanding. In addressing the challenge of literature and the arts to the church, Newman points out that the sources of these disciplines are diverse. They record and display the human condition, in its depravity as well as in its grandeur. This fact, he emphasizes, goes with the territory of Liberal Knowledge. Accept it as such, he counsels. Do not teach expurgated texts or put mental fig leaves on the nudes. Regarding literature, he advises, "Put up with it, as it is, or do not pretend to cultivate it. Take things as they are, not as you would wish them."[3] The church-related university, in sum, fears no form of knowledge. It represses no element of our nature. Rather, it "cultivates the whole."[4] "Right on!" we might agree, today.

If Newman were addressing my topic, "Catholic and Intellectual: Conjunction or Disjunction?" it is clear that his position would be "both/and" rather than one or the other. Well before the pessimism about reason, science, and technology brought on in the twentieth century by their blatant abuse by totalitarian despots and warmongers, Newman displays a keen sensitivity to the fact that Liberal Knowledge can be exploited, perverted, and applied to evil ends. The possession of Liberal Knowledge does not, in itself, make a person a better member of his or her faith community, a better person in God's sight. Thus, Newman posits a distinction between intellectual and moral virtue, insisting that they are not the same and that they do not automatically conduce to each other. At the same time, the church, and the church-related university committed to propagating Liberal Knowledge, must not fear, repress, censor, or subject to external criteria any of the arts or sciences. Such a university must cultivate all aspects of educational endeavor, acknowledging each discipline's distinctive ground rules, in order to cultivate the whole. In that respect, the copula in "Catholic and Intellectual" would be, for Newman, a conjunction as well as a disjunction. And, the disjunction, where it exists for him, speaks less to the limits of human reason than to the distinction he draws between intellectual and moral virtue.

I'd now like to turn to Pelikan's reconsideration of Newman. He speaks both as a professor and as a former graduate school dean. Just as there are features of Newman's outlook that reflect his historical situation and personal proclivities, so there are features of Pelikan's outlook that bespeak his personal experience and the general situation of American universities in the late twentieth century. Thus, Pelikan treats some issues—boards of trustees and their proper relations with university administrators and faculty, the responsibility of university presidents for sound fiscal management, intercollegiate athletics as big business with all the temptations thereunto appertaining—that are remote from Newman's purview. I plan to ignore these dimensions of Pelikan's essay, focusing instead on the areas in which his position can best be compared with Newman's, and best serve as a backdrop for my own reflections.

First, and in sharp contrast with Newman's rigorous distinction between intellectual and moral virtue, Pelikan thinks that universities must subscribe to and inculcate virtues that are both intellectual and moral. He heads the list with freedom of inquiry and intellectual honesty. Next, he observes, scholars have a moral as well as a professional duty to publish the results of their research, in a form, and a forum, where they can be evaluated by peers. What is at issue here, for Pelikan, is not just the duty of the professoriate to advance knowledge in addition to imparting it to their students. Nor is he seeking merely to develop an ethical rationale for the "publish or perish" policy of the research university. Beyond that, Pelikan argues that the willingness to subject one's work to peer review is a control and a corrective against intellectual hubris, self-satisfaction, and complacency. On this topic, Pelikan indicates that he is interested in the psychology of the professoriate, and the temptations confronting it, as much as he is in what a university education does for students. He makes a valid point, I think, in arguing that professors cannot be good role models for students unless they take intellectual risks and push the envelope themselves.

Thus, another intellectual virtue that is also a moral virtue for Pelikan is courage, the ability to stick to one's guns, if one is a revisionist or swimming against the current, and also the willingness to modify or abandon one's position if it is proved wrong, however large an ego investment one may have in one's older views. As with his point about submitting one's work to peer review, Pelikan's argument here stresses the humility and selflessness of the researcher in the quest for knowledge as a moral, and not just a professional, requirement. It also stresses the point that, in academia, authority is not ex officio; it is possessed only when it is earned, in the eyes of those competent to judge.

Pelikan certainly shares Newman's appreciation of the fact that different disciplines have their own procedures, methods, and criteria, and that members of a university must understand and respect that fact. But, once again, in addition to seeing this attitude as a moral no less than an intellectual virtue, Pelikan puts his own spin on the point. Unlike Newman, he does not focus on the responsibility to the disciplines of the university's administration, or of its chartering body. Rather, he focuses on academic collegiality. It is professors and students who have the duty to recognize both the pluralistic and the universalistic dimensions of human nature and experience. They must be able to distinguish between ideas which they may feel a duty to attack and the persons who articulate those ideas. For Pelikan, a central feature of the university's mission is

> to tolerate fundamental diversity of beliefs and values without sacrificing conviction. . . . What is needed is the skill and the art of holding views strongly and yet of respecting views that are diametrically opposed. This skill is one with which the university has had a rich experience. It involves a civility of discourse; . . . the discourse that goes on within the university may serve as the most impressive exhibit available to prove that civility is in fact the best means that human reason has devised . . . for coping with fundamental differences.[5]

I daresay that Pelikan's insistence on the importance of civility can be contextualized when we recall the frequent trashing of that virtue, in the academy and in society at large, since the 1960s. Had he been able to read Pelikan's book, I think that Newman would have found this insistence on civility both surprising and shocking. But, apart from his general claim that there are moral as well as intellectual virtues specific to the university's mission, Pelikan makes this observation about civility because he sees the university as the last bastion of rationality and courtesy in a world intellectually diminished by ideological bickering, the latest fads in cultural criticism, and the dumbing down of public discourse.

Going beyond that, Pelikan maintains that the virtues he sees as central to the university's mission are an integral part of ethics in general. They set the operative standards for us as academics, in whatever faith community we stand and in whatever kind of university we teach. In that sense, although Pelikan is not writing specifically about or for church-related universities, he does see the academic virtues as religiously significant, whatever an academic's personal convictions may be. I think that Pelikan makes a valid point here. I would agree that the integrity with which we do our work has a moral dimension, for all academics, and that it also has a religious dimension for those of us who place our professional labors in the framework of a divine reality that is our ultimate source of meaning. Pelikan is also concerned with how universities address the failure of some academics to uphold the intellectual and moral virtues of the academy, how they enforce academic freedom, and its flip side, academic responsibility. Thus, unlike Newman, Pelikan treats university governance, the legislation of principles and guidelines, both substantive and procedural, and their application, without fear or favor, to those who fall short. I would add a point here that Pelikan omits. Even the most cursory review of the horror stories in the *AAUP Journal* indicates that supra-university watchdog agencies and pressure groups also need to exist, to guard the on-campus guardians of academic freedom and responsibility.

Finally, although Pelikan writes about universities in general and not, specifically, about church-related universities, he does consider the relationship of the church to the university. On this subject, he takes a far bolder line than Newman. Pelikan argues that the church needs the university more than the university needs the church. And why? So that the church can understand its own message, the development of its own teachings and practices, and the ways in which they have been enculturated (to use a sociological term) or incarnated (to use a theological term) in different times and places. This understanding, in turn, is essential if the church is going to find the best ways to preach the Gospel in the present and future. To this end, Pelikan continues, the church needs the help of many university disciplines. It needs linguistic and philological expertise, which enable it to reconstruct and interpret its foundation documents. It needs history, comparative religion, psychology, and the social sciences, which help the church understand the development of its theology in context. I would concur. For we are educating students to understand their own traditions, and all vital and durable traditions are complex, in their histories, and multiform, in their modes of praxis. We are also educating students to be citizens of a pluralistic society; thus they need to have a knowledge and understanding of other people's religious traditions. In the case of students who are Catholics, we need to prepare them to embrace the ecumenical imperatives of Vatican II. To return to Pelikan, he adds that the church also needs philosophy and the sciences, which give it a vocabulary enabling it to make its theology comprehensible and defensible in the intellectual community.

In making this point, Pelikan speaks to two historical facts which I would corroborate: First, for the most part, universities today no longer depend on churches as their sponsors. And, in the case of universities that do, they are on notice that the church-related university is not the only game in town. In order to hold up their heads with pride, such universities have to subscribe to the same intellectual values and, in Pelikan's case, virtues that define the university as such. If not, their personnel will simply move elsewhere and make their pedagogy available in contexts not subject to ecclesiastical oversight. Second, ecclesiastical traditions have never been static or monolithic. They have always embraced multiple interpretations of authority and they have had to reinvent themselves repeatedly in order to "speak to" different cultures and mind-sets. Pelikan emphasizes the point that churches need what university education can supply since, as the vehicles of living traditions, they must undergo development lest they atrophy. In sum, Pelikan weaves into the theme of the church's need for the university a master pattern: Newman's own view of the development of doctrine.

I find that both Newman and Pelikan offer us much food for thought. If Newman is prophetic in his skepticism about the automatic application of Liberal Knowledge to good causes, Pelikan's confidence that intellectual virtues are moral virtues also rings true, even though he wisely qualifies the point by recognizing that professors share the temptations of fallen humanity: they may be vain, proud, envious, manipulative, and selfish. In addition to acculturation, universities need to provide clear academic ground rules in order to thwart these proclivities and, at worst, to penalize them. Both authors emerge as realists. Neither is suckered by the Enlightenment myth of the inevitable march of progress through reason and science. Both see a place for theology in the intellectual discourse of the university; both see the university as standing above and apart from theology as confessional drumbeating, masquerading as scholarship. Both treat theology as a humanistic discipline operating under the same academic ground rules as other humanistic disciplines. Both consider the church in relation to the university. Newman sees the church-related university as having a *duty* to support Liberal Knowledge; Pelikan sees the church, whether in church-supported universities or not, as having a *need* for the university's support. As I see it, both perspectives have merit, and they do not contradict each other. Finally, both Newman and Pelikan are aware of the fact that the defense of academic freedom and the respect for the independence of the scholarly disciplines, values defining the modern university in whatever setting, derive from the medieval university. I agree with that idea but, as a medievalist, I would amplify it, arguing that the medieval university can best be understood as the culmination, for its time, of a longer historical tradition that goes back to the early church. Church-related universities are, historically, the primogenitary heirs of that tradition and should be its strongest defenders, however much some of them may try to ignore that legacy, and however much external influences may seek to induce memory loss.

The medieval model begins in the patristic period. Initially, early Christians sent their children to the state-supported schools of liberal arts, rather than setting up a parallel educational system conveying literacy in Greek and Latin with bowdlerized versions of classical authors. As a product and exponent of the classical school, St. Augustine, considering the education men preparing to be biblical exegetes and preachers would need, included the entire classical curriculum, omitting astrology alone. With respect to these cultural riches, he advises his students to "spoil the Egyptians of their gold and silver" as they bring it into the Promised Land.[6] By the sixth century, the state-supported classical schools were gone in the wake of the Roman Empire. The locus of schooling in the liberal arts shifted to monasteries. The prevailing spirit of the new monastic schoolmasters is summed up well by Cassiodorus. Reflecting on the role of the classics in monastic education, he expresses the firm conviction that the preservation of liberal culture is a responsibility of Christian educators: "May the task of the ancients be our task,"[7] he exhorts his readers. Picking up on the same theme, the twelfth-century educator Hugh of St. Victor proposes, "Learn everything. You will see afterwards that nothing is superfluous. A skimpy knowledge is not a pleasing thing,"[8] in the model curriculum of arts and sciences he drafted for the neophyte biblical scholars of his own day.

The same century in which Hugh wrote saw the first emergence of the universities and of the scholastic method that flourished there. Notwithstanding the episcopal umbrella under which most early universities arose, by the early thirteenth century, if not before, they had acquired corporate liberties freeing them from the control of church and state alike. As autonomous corporations, universities, and their subcorporations in individual faculties, determined their own curricula, the requirements for degrees, the ways of testing the competence of candidates for them, and the modes of policing their own ranks. On the few occasions when popes or princes tried to intervene and prescribe loyalty tests, the influence of these external authorities was generally nugatory; at most, it shifted the action, or some personnel, to other university centers. In practice, as in principle, universities defended and institutionalized the twelfth-century precept defining intellectual life: *diversi, sed non adversi.*[9] In all faculties, from the arts curriculum to the postgraduate fields of medicine, law, and theology, there were always several masters teaching the same subjects, each with his own interpretation of the material. It was acknowledged that unity did not require uniformity; a plurality of positions could coexist within the orthodox consensus, even in the high-risk fields of theology and canon law. In working out their individual positions, scholastics in all fields developed a critical method, based on the consideration of reason and authority alike. They felt free, even obliged, to analyze the foundation documents within their disciplines, applying logical, historical, and philosophical criticism to bear on them, deciding which authorities remained pertinent and which needed to be contextualized, relativized, put on the shelf, or even rejected. Even while advocating rival solutions to the same problems, medieval academics could preserve collegiality, and a strong sense of their collective identity, despite the argumentative style that marked scholastic debate.

It is out of this tradition that we derive our treasured right of academic freedom and our commitment to intellectual courage and honesty, our respect for colleagues in different disciplines, as well as for the work of colleagues in our own fields with whom we disagree. These are values to which both Newman and Pelikan speak. It is out of this tradition, as well, that the concept of academic responsibility derives: our duty to uphold standards, our duty not to turn the power of the podium in our classrooms into a bully pulpit, our duty not to debase the teacher-student relationship into a relationship of guru and groupie. This is the legacy that we all inherit. The Catholic university and the Catholic professoriate inherit it in particular. We have the obligation to embody and defend it, whatever kinds of colleges and universities may employ us. Whatever our affiliations, we also have the obligation to be good citizens of our academic communities, recognizing that eternal vigilance is the price of liberty, academic and otherwise. This may mean that we have to remind our colleagues, our administrators, and the ecclesiastical bodies to which they report in some cases, that they, too, have a duty to be faithful to the tradition of the medieval university that is their own richest inheritance. If they are laggard in that duty, if they try to dismiss it as passé, we have the responsibility to recall them to it, to embarrass them for neglecting it, and even to hold their collective feet to the fire, if necessary. It is to be hoped that drastic action of this sort will not be required. For if Catholic academics are clear about these values and solid in their willingness to promote them and to hold their leaders accountable to them, we can keep the flag aloft. After all, without us, neither the church nor the university can carry out its educational mission. For me, therefore, the motto which that flag proudly proclaims is: Catholic *and* Intellectual: Conjunction *not* Disjunction!

CHAPTER 6

Catholicism and Human Rights

MARY ANN GLENDON

I am deeply honored to have been chosen for this year's Marianist Award. And I was delighted when Father Heft told me I could give this lecture on any aspect of my work, so long as I included a discussion of how my faith has affected my scholarship and how my scholarship has affected my faith. At the time, that sounded like an easy assignment, since it was the experience of representing the Holy See at a United Nations conference that led to the book I have just completed—a history of the Universal Declaration of Human Rights of 1948, combined with a biography of Eleanor Roosevelt for the years when she presided over the drafting of that document.[1] The more I thought about Father Heft's request to say something about how my faith has affected my scholarship and vice versa, however, the more I realized that it is not at all simple to trace those connections.

So I decided that I should probably begin with a few words about what led me into international studies in the first place. As I look back, it seems to me that the much-maligned Latin liturgy of my youth had a lot to do with it. Perhaps only someone who happened to grow up in a small town can understand me when I say that for me, in rural western Massachusetts of the 1950s, the pre–Vatican II Church was a brightly colored window opening out to the great world of people, places, events, and ideas that lay beyond Berkshire County. The Sunday missal, with Latin on one page and the English translation facing it, not only got me interested in languages, but gave me a sense of being linked to people all over the earth—people who were reading the same words in the same language as I was, but who lived in places where it never snowed, or in great cities like Rome, Dublin, and New York, or countries behind the mysterious "iron curtain."

I have to trace my inclination for comparative studies back to those days, too, because even though my home town had only five thousand people, it contained two very different cultures: the world of my Irish Catholic father and his relatives and the Yankee Congregationalist world of my mother's family. As a result of their rather daring mixed marriage, my brother and sister and I were more or less forced to become little theologians. We tried to figure out the answers to such perplexing questions as whether our mother and father could both go to Heaven, and, if so, whether that would be the same Heaven.

In my teenage years, I began to encounter even more questions that I could not answer on the basis of what I had learned in Sunday school. Like many people, I began to put religion in one mental compartment and high learning into another. I am sure that I do not have to tell anyone here that the transition from one's childhood faith to a more mature spirituality is a road filled with potholes. And I fell into my share of them.

But what prevented me from locking religion into a sealed cranial chamber forever were three circumstances that also had a good deal of influence on my scholarship later on. The first was that, as a high school student, quite by chance, I came across an essay in our local newspaper by Father Theodore Hesburgh, then the president of Notre Dame. One sentence jumped out at me. It was like a message in a bottle that washed up on the seashore just when I needed it. It was this: "When you encounter a conflict between science and religion, you're either dealing with a bad scientist or a bad theologian." It's no exaggeration to say that sentence had an enormous effect on my life by stimulating me to think *critically* about the natural and human sciences alike.

I am glad that I had the opportunity, many years later, to meet Father Ted and tell him how much that sentence of his had meant to me. By that time, his words had been reinforced by the work of the late Bernard Lonergan, who did so much to help Catholics to remain in dialogue with the natural and human sciences. Lonergan encourages us to follow the example of Thomas Aquinas, who, utterly unafraid of where his God-given intellect would lead him, did not hesitate to engage the thought of great pagan philosophers.

The second factor that kept me from building a mental firewall between faith and reason was that I happened to attend the University of Chicago at a time when its leading intellectual lights held Catholic thought in exceptionally high esteem. The curriculum had been designed by Robert Maynard Hutchins, who often said how much he admired the Church for having the longest intellectual tradition of any institution in the world. He and Mortimer Adler drew heavily from that tradition when they constructed Chicago's famous Great Books program. So heavily in fact, that Chicago was often described as the place where atheist professors taught Thomas Aquinas to Marxist students.

My Chicago education in Catholic philosophy, however, did not extend to Catholic social thought. In fact, I managed to get all the way through college without the slightest awareness that there was such a thing, though I had read and been deeply impressed by the autobiography of Dorothy Day.[2] What changed that was a third circumstance: the Second Vatican Council. It would be impossible to exaggerate the electrifying effect that John XXIII and the Second Vatican Council had on me and other young Catholics who were just beginning to make our way in the world in the early 1960s.

So, all in all, it is perhaps not surprising that I gravitated, as a lawyer, to international and comparative studies, to human rights, and to areas of law that correspond to major topics of Catholic social thought. And that brings me to the main subject I'd like to discuss with you today: the interesting reciprocal relationship between Catholic social thought and the post–World War II human rights project that I discovered in the course of digging into the origins of the United Nations Universal Declaration of Human Rights of 1948.

CATHOLIC INFLUENCES ON THE HUMAN RIGHTS PROJECT

If you are like most Americans, and like me before I got interested in the Universal Declaration, you probably do not stay up nights thinking about the United Nations and its various pronouncements. So let me begin with a little background on the Universal Declaration, and why it seemed to me to be worth studying. During World War II, the idea began to percolate that there should be some kind of international bill of rights—a common standard to which all nations could aspire—and by which they could measure their own and each others' progress.

One of the first suggestions came from Pope Pius XII, who called in a June 1941 radio address for an international bill recognizing the rights that flowed from the dignity of the person.[3] Another came from the British writer H. G. Wells in a little pamphlet subtitled *What Are We Fighting For?*[4] But in practical terms, the most consequential support came from several Latin American countries, who comprised twenty-one of the original fifty-five member nations of the UN when it was founded in 1945.

It was largely due to the insistence of the Latin Americans, joined by other small nations, that the UN established a Human Rights Commission, composed of members from eighteen different countries. It was chaired by Eleanor Roosevelt, who was just then making a new life for herself after the death of her husband. (The title of my book, *A World Made New*, is taken from a prayer that Mrs. Roosevelt used to carry in her purse, and I chose it to evoke not only the aspirations of the framers of the Declaration in the postwar period, but also the changes that were taking place in her own life.)

When the Human Rights Commission set to work in early 1947, its first major task was to draft a "bill of rights" to which persons of all nations and cultures could subscribe. But that assignment rested upon a couple of problematic assumptions: no one really knew whether there were any such common principles, or what they might be. So UNESCO asked a group of philosophers—some well known in the West, like Jacques Maritain, and others from Confucian, Hindu, and Muslim countries—to examine the question. These philosophers sent a questionnaire to still more leading thinkers all over the world, from Mahatma Gandhi to Teilhard de Chardin, and in due course they reported that, somewhat to their surprise, they had found that there were a few common standards of decency that were widely shared, though not always formulated in the language of rights. Their conclusion was that this practical consensus was enough to enable the project to go forward.

The judgment of the philosophers was borne out by the experience of the delegates on the Human Rights Commission. This group, too, was highly diverse, but they had few disagreements over the content of the Declaration. Their disputes were chiefly political, and chiefly involved the Soviet Union and the United States hurling accusations of hypocrisy against each other.

On December 10, 1948, the document was adopted by the UN General Assembly as a "common standard of achievement." There were no dissenting votes, although the Soviet bloc, Saudi Arabia, and South Africa recorded abstentions. The Declaration quickly became the principal inspiration of the postwar international human rights movement; the model for the majority of rights instruments in the world—over ninety in all; and it serves today as the single most important reference point for discussions of human rights in international settings.

But the more the human rights idea caught on, the fiercer became the contests over the meanings of the provisions of the Declaration. So, after returning from the Beijing Women's Conference, I decided to read up a bit on the original understanding of the Declaration. I expected to just go to the library and check out a book or two. But to my surprise, there were no histories of the framing at that time, apart from three doctoral theses, all done at European universities. So I began to read the primary sources myself.

It did not take long to realize that the framers of the UDHR (Universal Declaration of Human Rights), like legal drafters everywhere, had done a good deal of copying. They drew many provisions from existing constitutions and rights instruments that the staff of the UN Human Rights Division had collected from all over the world. They relied most heavily of all on two draft proposals for international bills that were themselves based on extensive cross-national research. One of these proposals was prepared under the auspices of the American Law Institute, and the other was a Latin American document that became the 1948 Bogota Declaration of the Rights and Duties of Man.

The final draft produced by Mrs. Roosevelt's commission was a synthesis drawn from many sources—and thus a document that differed in many ways from our familiar Anglo-American rights instruments—most noticeably in its inclusion of social and economic rights, and in its express acknowledgment that rights are subject to duties and limitations. It also differed from socialist charters, notably with its strong emphasis on political and civil liberties.

Several features of the Declaration set it apart from *both* Anglo-American and Soviet bloc documents. Consider the following: its pervasive emphasis on the "inherent dignity" and "worth of the human person"; the affirmation that the human person is "endowed with reason and conscience"; the right to form trade unions; the worker's right to just remuneration for himself and his family; the recognition of the family as the "natural and fundamental group unit of society" entitled as such to "protection by society and the state"; the prior right of parents to choose the education of their children; and a provision that motherhood and childhood are entitled to "special care and assistance."[5]

Where did those ideas come from? The immediate source was the twentieth-century constitutions of many Latin American and continental European countries. But where did the Latin Americans and continental Europeans get them? The proximate answer to that question is: mainly from the programs of political parties, parties of a type that did not exist in the United States, Britain, or the Soviet bloc, namely, Christian Democratic and Christian Social parties.

But where did the politicians get *their* ideas about the family, work, civil society, and the dignity of the person? The answer to that is: mainly from the social encyclicals *Rerum Novarum* (1891) and *Quadragesimo Anno* (1931). And where did the Church get them? The short answer is that those encyclicals were part of the process through which the Church had begun to reflect on the Enlightenment, the eighteenth-century revolutions, socialism, and the labor question in the light of Scripture, tradition, and her own experience as an "expert in humanity."[6]

The most articulate advocate of this whole complex of ideas on the Human Rights Commission was a Lebanese Arab of the Greek

Orthodox faith, Charles Malik. In reading the old UN transcripts, I was struck by Malik's frequent use of terms like the "intermediate associations" of civil society, and by his emphatic preference for the term "person" rather than "individual." When I had the opportunity to meet Charles Malik's son, Dr. Habib Malik, I asked Dr. Malik if he knew where his father had acquired that vocabulary. The answer was: from the heavily underlined copies of *Rerum Novarum* and *Quadragesimo Anno* which Malik kept among the books he most frequently consulted. Charles Malik thus seems to have been one of the first of an impressive line of non-Catholic intellectuals who found a treasure trove of ideas in Catholic social teaching.

The most zealous promoters of social and economic rights, contrary to what is now widely supposed, were not the Soviet bloc representatives, but delegates from the Latin American countries. Except for the Mexican delegates, most of these people were inspired not by Marx and Engels but by Leo XIII and Pius XI. Their focus was not on the exploitation of man by man, but on the dignity of work and the preferential option for the poor.

The Latin American influence continued when the Human Rights Commissioners submitted their draft Declaration for final review by a large UN committee composed of representatives from all the member nations. In 1948, the Latin Americans were still the largest single group in the UN. And they used their clout. They offered so many amendments that they incurred the wrath of the Canadian lawyer who was then serving as the director of the UN Division of Human Rights.

In a memoir published many years later, John Humphrey referred to the Latin American efforts to bring in still more ideas from their own 1948 draft Declaration as "the Bogota Menace." Of the group's Cuban spokesman, he said, "Highly intelligent, Guy Perez Cisneros used every procedural device to reach his end. His speeches were laced with Roman Catholic social philosophy, and it seemed at times that the chief protagonists in the conference room were the Roman Catholics and the communists, with the latter a poor second."[7] In his private diaries, published after his death, Humphrey was less circumspect in recounting his reactions. There, he described Cisneros as a man who "combines demagogy with Roman Catholic social philosophy," and said that Cisneros "should burn in hell" for holding up the proceedings with his calls for amendments.[8]

I think I have said enough to show that the contributions of Catholic social thought to the Universal Declaration were far from insignificant. But to avoid any misunderstanding, let me emphasize again that this was just one of many sources of influence on that impressively multicultural document.

Now I would like to turn to a consideration of some of the ways in which that influence was reciprocated.

THE INFLUENCE OF THE UNIVERSAL HUMAN RIGHTS IDEA ON CATHOLICISM

Here the trail is harder to follow, but I believe it begins in Paris in 1948 when the Human Rights Commissioners were trying to round up support from as many nations as possible for the final vote on the Declaration in the UN General Assembly. A key figure in that lobbying process was the French member of the Commission, René Cassin. Cassin was a distinguished French lawyer who described himself as a secular Jew. He had lost twenty-nine relatives in concentration camps, and was later to win the Nobel Peace Prize for his human rights activities. There is an intriguing sentence in Cassin's memoirs where he says that in the fall of 1948 he was aided on several occasions by the "discreet personal encouragements" of the Papal Nuncio in Paris.[9] That Nuncio was none other than Angelo Roncalli, the future Pope John XXIII.

Roncalli's subsequent actions suggest that events in the UN that fall must have made a great impression on him. It also seems clear that he must have agreed with Maritain and other Catholic thinkers that there was value in discussing certain human goods as rights, even though the biblical tradition uses the language of obligation. In *Pacem in Terris*, John XXIII referred to the Universal Declaration by name and called it "an act of the highest importance."[10]

Many Catholics were surprised, and some were even shocked, at the extent to which the documents of Vatican II, and John XXIII's encyclicals *Pacem in Terris* and *Mater et Magistra*, seemed to reflect a shift from natural law to human rights.[11] Some writers regard this shift as mainly rhetorical, an effort on the part of the Church to make her teachings intelligible to "all men and women of good will."[12]

But I believe it was more than that. I would say it was also part of the Church's shift from nature to history, as well as her increasing openness to learning from other traditions. The Church has always taught, with St. Paul, that our knowledge of truth in this life is imperfect; that "now we see only as in a mirror dimly." But she has not always been so forceful as John Paul II was in *Centesimus Annus* when he insisted that Christian believers are obliged to remain open to discover "every fragment of truth . . . in the life experience and in the culture of individuals and nations."[13] A hallmark of the thought of John Paul II has been his sense of being in partnership with all of humanity in a shared quest for a better apprehension of truth.

With hindsight, we can see that Vatican II only marked the beginning of the Church's appropriation of modern rights discourse.[14] As one of the younger Council Fathers, Bishop Karol Wojtyla from Krakow shared John XXIII's appreciation of the postwar human rights project. John Paul II has repeatedly praised the Universal Declaration of Human Rights, calling it "one of the highest expressions of the human conscience of our time" and "a real milestone on the path of the moral progress of humanity."[15]

Needless to say, the Church's adoption of rights language entailed the need to be very clear about the fact that she does not always use that terminology in the same way it is used in secular circles. Those who think the Church should never have gone down that road at all often fail to notice two important facts about the Church's use of rights language. First, the rights tradition into which the Church has tapped is the biblically informed, continental, dignitarian tradition which she herself had already done so much to shape. "The Catholic doctrine of human rights," Avery Dulles points out, "is not based on Lockean empiricism or individualism. It has a more ancient and distinguished pedigree."[16]

Second, the Church did not even uncritically adopt the dignitarian vision. In *Gaudium et Spes*, the Council Fathers say that the movement to respect human rights "must be imbued with the spirit of the Gospel and be protected from all appearance of mistaken auton-omy. We are tempted to consider our personal rights as fully protected only when we are free from every norm of divine law; but following this road leads to the destruction rather than to the maintenance of the dignity of the human person."[17] In the same vein, John XXIII noted in *Pacem in Terris* that everything the Church says about human rights is conditioned by their foundation in the dignity that attaches to the person made in the image and likeness of God, and everything is oriented to the end of the common good. And when John Paul II sent his good wishes to the UN on the occasion of the fiftieth anniver-sary of the Declaration in 1998, he challenged the assembly with these words: "Inspired by the example of all those who have taken the *risk of freedom*, can we not recommit ourselves also to taking the *risk of solidarity*—and thus the *risk of peace?*"[18]

Some of the most striking interactions between Catholic social thought and human rights have occurred in the field of international advocacy. With over 300,000 educational, health care, and relief agen-cies serving mainly the world's poorest inhabitants, the Church has become an outspoken advocate of social justice in international set-tings. But it is a hard sell. Challenging passages like this one from the 1997 World Day of Peace message do not sit particularly well with affluent nations and first-world interest groups:

> Living out [the] demanding commitment [to solidarity] requires a total reversal of the alleged values which make people seek only their own good: power, pleasure, the unscrupulous accumulation of wealth. . . . A society of genuine solidarity can be built only if the well-off in helping the poor, do not stop at giving from what they do not need. Those living in poverty can wait no longer: They need help now and so have a *right* to receive immediately what they need [emphasis supplied].

At first glance, words like "a right to receive what one needs" sound uncomfortably like simplistic, secular social advocacy. But the Church's use of rights language in this context cannot be equated with crude mandates for state-run, social-engineering programs. For one thing, the Church has always refrained from proposing specific models: her gift to political science has been, rather, the principle of subsidiarity—which is steadily attracting interest in the secular world.

Moreover, the Church teaches solidarity not as a policy, but as a *virtue*—a virtue which inclines us to overcome sources of division within ourselves and within society. Like any other virtue, solidarity requires constant practice; it is inseparable from personal reform.

The Church's advocacy for the preferential option for the poor has led her to become a staunch defender of the Universal Declaration as an integrated whole. While most nations take a selective approach to human rights, the Holy See consistently lifts up the original vision of the Declaration—a vision in which political and civil rights are indispensable for social and economic justice, and vice versa. At a time when affluent nations seem increasingly to be washing their hands of poor countries and peoples, it is often the Holy See, and only the Holy See, that keeps striving to bring together the two halves of the divided soul of the human rights project—its resounding affirmation of freedom and its insistence on one human family for which all bear a common responsibility.

As for the future, I believe the dialogue between Catholicism and the human rights tradition will continue, and that it will be beneficial to both. One may even imagine that the resources of the Catholic tradition may be helpful in resolving several thorny dilemmas that have bedeviled the human rights project from its outset, especially the dilemmas arising from challenges to its universality and its truth claims. A fuller exposition of that point would require another lecture, but let me briefly sketch some ways in which Catholic thinkers might be helpful with regard to these problems.

Take for example the dilemma of how there can be universal rights in view of the diversity among cultures which has recently resurfaced with a vengeance. A number of Asian and Islamic leaders (unlike the Asian and Islamic representatives on the original Human Rights Commission) take the position that all rights are culturally relative. They claim that so-called universal rights are really just instruments of Western cultural imperialism.

The long Catholic experience in the dialectic between the core teachings of the faith and the various cultural settings in which the

faith has been received helps us to see that to accept universal principles does not mean accepting that they must be brought to life in
the same way everywhere. The experience of Catholicism with the
inculturation of its basic teachings shows that universality need not
entail homogeneity. In fact the whole Church has been enriched by
the variety of ways in which the faith has been expressed around the
world.

The framers of the Universal Declaration of Human Rights had
similar expectations for the relatively short list of rights that they
deemed fundamental. Their writings reveal that they contemplated a
legitimate pluralism in forms of freedom, a variety of means of protecting basic rights, and different ways of resolving the tensions among
rights, provided that no rights were completely subordinated to others.
As Jacques Maritain put it, there can be many different kinds of music
played on the Declaration's thirty strings.

It seems unfortunate that that pluralist understanding has been
almost completely forgotten, even by friends of the human rights project. For the more that Western groups promote a top-down, homoge-
nizing vision of human rights, the more credibility they add to the
charge of Western cultural imperialism.

Another dilemma for the human rights project is the challenge of
historicism and relativism. If there are no common truths to which all
men and women can appeal, then there are no human rights, and
there is little hope that reason and choice can prevail over force and
accident in the realm of human affairs. It is one thing to acknowledge
that the human mind can glimpse truth only as though a glass darkly;
and quite another to deny the existence of truth altogether. Hannah
Arendt has warned that "The ideal subject of totalitarian rule is not
the convinced Nazi or the convinced Communist, but people for
whom the distinction between fact and fiction . . . and the distinction
between true and false . . . no longer exist."[19]

At a time when much of the postmodern secular academy seems
to have given up on reason and the search for truth, it is heartening to
read the spirited defense of reason in the encyclical *Fides et Ratio*.
The "reason" that the Church defends is not the calculating reason
of Hobbes, in the service of the passions, nor is it narrow scientific

rationalism. It is the dynamic, recurrent, and potentially self-correcting process of experiencing, understanding, and judging that has animated her best theologians from Thomas Aquinas to Bernard Lonergan.

I trust that my enthusiasm for Catholic social thought and philosophy will not be understood as unbridled boosterism. I am well aware that much of what our tradition has to offer was learned painfully after mistakes and sad experience.

On the other hand, there is such a thing as exaggerated self-criticism. At a time, and in a culture, where the Church is under siege from many directions, I believe that Catholic intellectuals do a great disservice when they contribute to the myth that the history of Christianity in general and Catholicism in particular is a history of patriarchy, worldliness, persecution, or exclusion of people or ideas. When I hear these rants against the Church, I always find it helpful to ask: Compared to what?

My own consciousness on that subject was raised by my Jewish husband who, like my teachers at the University of Chicago, has a great admiration for Catholicism. He often tells me he just can't understand why so many Catholics just roll over when their Church is unfairly attacked, or why they do not take pride in her great accomplishments.

However that may be, it is good to know that there are still many institutions of higher learning where the Catholic intellectual tradition remains in lively dialogue with the natural and human sciences and with other faiths. From all that I have heard, the University of Dayton is one of the places where that great conversation continues. I am profoundly grateful to have been asked to be a part of that conversation on this occasion where you celebrate and renew the Marianist tradition.

CHAPTER 7

A Feeling for Hierarchy

MARY DOUGLAS

To receive the Marianist Award is a great honor. For the occasion I am asked to say something about the influence of my religious faith on my work, or about the interaction of one with the other. This is perhaps a straightforward assignment for a person whose work has been involved with the direction of public affairs. But it is less easy for an anthropologist, partly because it means delving into fairly intimate thoughts as you will see, and partly because of this particular religion, the Roman Catholic faith.

I once asked Fredrik Barth, the Norwegian anthropologist and Islamicist, whether the day would come when Catholicism would be accorded by ethnographers the same benevolence as is given to Judaism, Hinduism, and Islam, or to African religions. He replied, "I doubt it, there is too much history." I knew what he meant. For nearly two millennia the Roman Catholic Church enjoyed the benefits of powerful imperial backing. Anthropologists can present other religions as ethnic victims of Western hegemony, and local versions of Catholicism can pass if they are practiced in Latin America or other very poor countries. But otherwise it is apt to be subject to radical criticism. Thus inhibited, I thought to make it less personal, I chose the idea of hierarchy as a central theme.[1]

When I say "hierarchy," I am remembering that the Roman Catholic Church calls herself a hierarchy. Sometimes she goes through a sectarian phase of withdrawal behind battlements, and at all times she has honored personal ecstatic experience. But in her own estimation she is a great, inclusive, ordered hierarchy, with graded units from newly baptized parishioner to pope. This distinctive feature contrasts with many other Christian churches, though not with all.

Preparing for this lecture I realize that I have always been attracted to hierarchy. I have also recognized that my good feelings toward it are countercultural. But then, I am not defining it as a soulless bureaucracy. I see it as a spontaneously created and maintained inclusive system, organizing its internal tensions by balance and symmetry, and rich in resources for peace and reconciliation. I miss it when it is not there, and grieve when it falls into any of its besetting traps.

The bad meanings currently associated with hierarchy amount to so much prejudice in the other direction that the sinologist Benjamin Schwartz declared it practically impossible for a modern scholar to understand an ancient oriental civilization.[2] I get teased for my kindly feeling for hierarchy. Friends consider that their own attitudes are based on a liberal dislike of tyranny, unlike my stuffy and illiberal prejudices. It is true that I tend to smell disorder afar off and to feel baffled when my friends rejoice at the thought of things falling into chaos. My sense that authority is vulnerable and needs support appalled a young Chinese political scientist in California in the 1970s. "Mary! How *can* you feel sorry for authority!"

The anti-hierarchical attitude is just as much a product of cultural bias as the pro-hierarchical, so culture became my abiding interest. Hierarchy is the encompassing principle of order which systematizes any field of work, whether a library, a game, an alphabet, mathematics, systematics of all kinds. What I find interesting is that there should be such strong feelings against a principle that must be present to some extent in any organization whatever. There can be human associations which are entirely haphazard and unorganized, like passengers on a bus, but the least bit of organization implies a reference to the whole, to a larger system of which the social unit is a part.

If I have to describe a hierarchical culture in a few words, I would start with what it is not. Hierarchy is *not* a vertical command structure dominated by an up-down pattern of communication. It is not a system requiring unquestioning deference to arbitrary fiats issued from above. Though that may be the current popular usage, Max Weber was on the mark when he emphasized the rational ordering and universalizing principles of bureaucracy. The glaring contrast with hierarchy is the pragmatic culture of individualism: there you do find up-down command systems, like ladders for individuals to climb on, and to jump off onto another one when it suits. Individualism has a philosophy of equality and a practice of inequality based on power and wealth. In an individualist system nothing is fixed, neither rank nor power; it is very competitive. It holds great personal sorrows (anyone may at any time be forced down, or out, according to the competition), and great joys for individual winners.

But hierarchy restricts competition, it institutes authority. Its institutions work to prevent concentrations of power. It is a positional system in which everyone has a place, every place has a prescribed trajectory of roles through time, in total the pattern of positions is coherent and the roles are coordinated. In place of the surprises and inexplicable disappointments suffered in a culture of individualism, those living in a hierarchy are exposed to the sadnesses of frustration and neglect of their talents, but at least there is a rational explanation.

MY GRANDPARENTS' HOME

Born in 1921, I first experienced hierarchy in a very modest form in my grandparents' home, and then in my convent schooling. So used to it was I that when I left school I was at a loss to understand what was happening around me. Only after the war, when I started anthropology in 1946, did I begin to understand. Reading anthropologists' monographs, I recognized hierarchy as a control on competition in the structure of checks and balances, for example, in the Ashanti constitution, and in West African ancestral cults. When I came to do my own fieldwork in the (Belgian) Congo I was puzzled by the absence of lineages and ancestors. Up-down hierarchy would seem to be present at the level of family life, with the seniority and authority of the father or grandfather, but it was always modified by distancing rules that protected the junior members from possibly tyrannous seniors. I saw varied ways of dispersing power, trying to maintain stability, principles of fairness controlling willful individuals.

Hierarchy is a pivotal issue for my understanding of social theory; at the same time my religious commitment endows the topic with passionate interest. For me, this is the point of interchange between religion and learning, and I should explain how my strong interest is founded in infant and early experience. We were left with my grandparents when I was five and my sister was three years old. What was called "Sending home the children" was a normal part of British colonial family life. It was backed by a theory that white children would not be able to survive the rigors of the tropics.[3] My father was in the Indian Civil Service in Burma. He got "home leave" every three years, and my mother came back to see us every year.

Living with grandparents is living in a hierarchy. Between this middle-aged couple all the important questions have been settled long ago. There are no disputes, no bad language, no mention of money in front of the children or servants. There are little mysteries, no one knows what they do not need to know, and nothing is quite what it seems. My grandfather is the nominal head of the house, but nobody could doubt that my grandmother is the person really in control. Inside the house is her sphere; outside is his.

The space of the house (a bungalow in Devon) was divided according to social categories. In 1926 every one had maids. The privacy of the maids' bedrooms was respected; no one could penetrate into that space except the cook and the house-parlor maid. The same for the nanny's bedroom. Nor did anyone enter the grandparents' bedroom without being invited. The maid cleaned the main bathroom but she did not use it, nor did the cook or the nanny. The maids and the children used a little attic bathroom. These rules of respect in space did not apply to the children's bedroom or playroom; they were too young to have a person's full rights to privacy. Of course the maid went into the grown-ups' public spaces as part of her duties, but I never saw her sit on a chair in the dining room, smoking room, or drawing room. Children only entered these rooms at set times and under supervision. Food was patterned to correspond to the time of day, the day of the week, and the calendar of annual holidays. As to justice, "No favoritism" was the general rule of impartiality, sharing was the rule of distribution, but as the elder I often got priority.

In seven years of caring for us, neither of our grandparents ever broke ranks to confide in us, one against the other, and we never told tales on each other. It was unthinkable. My first, limited, experience of hierarchy was a life organized as a system of temporal and spatial positions, held in balance by mutual respect. It was the same later, at the French convent primary school in Torquay. The sense of pattern was reassuring, given the basic insecurity of being separated from our parents. At that stage I just knew it by living it. And the life framed by hierarchical practice continued until I was twelve. The experience was organized but inarticulate; the practice was not put into words. Today I am trying to articulate it.

HIERARCHICAL PRINCIPLES

I now think of my early experiences of hierarchy in terms of ten principles. The five that I list here correspond quite well to my grand-parents' house, but later I will need to list five more that are elaborations of these.

1. Hierarchy is a pattern of positions given in physical and social terms.

2. Competition would mess up the carefully worked out system; competition is restricted, disapproved from below as well as from above.

3. The top position is more ritual than effective, or political. Power is so diffused that the husband, chief, or king has little of it. In this sense it is not what is known as patriarchal.

4. Control of information protects stability. Communication in a hierarchy is characterized by forbidden words, silences and secrets.

5. The top level of authority must never fail to respect the lowest.

In my grandmother's house these principles were learned by living according to precepts. I call it my grandmother's, not my grandfather's house because in the domestic sphere she was supreme. My grand-father had a sphere of his own to which she had no access; he belonged to a social club (male members only) in Totnes, and was a local magis-trate. He was representative of the family in external relations, paying the taxes for example. Within the house he was a cypher, nominal head, the ritual personage to whom deference was paid, but who had no commanding voice. Thus was the house organized by gender.

No competition was allowed between my sister and myself; for many purposes I had the formal precedence due to age, two years ahead of her. But the general rule was equality between us; we were expected to share presents. Respect for the maids by not entering their rooms and not reprimanding them except in the kitchen was a mild version of the respect for junior ranks. There was such marked asymmetry between employer and employed that the downward communication line was stronger than the upward one. If offended the maid or cook or nanny might threaten to leave, a powerful weapon indeed, and a continual subject of conversation between my grandmother and her friends.

RULES

When I was twelve, everything changed. My mother died. My father retired from Burma, and set up house for us. We left our grandparents to go to live with him, a kindly stranger who had never had much to do with children. Headed by a widower, the house was not gendered; there were no resident maids. But the dual principle of hierarchy was present in fractured form on account of the fact that we, the young daughters, were Catholics. My father was invincibly agnostic, but he made it his pious duty to drive us to Mass and the three of us put flowers on my mother's grave every Sunday without fail. As to religion we had the sectarian sense of superiority instilled by our first convent school.

At this point we went to the boarding school at Roehampton that was made infamous by the title of Antonia White's novel, *Frost in May*. It was the Sacred Heart Convent that my mother herself had gone to when she had been "sent home," and her cousins too, also "sent home" from the tropics. Several of the nuns had been educated there too. Dying, she formally entrusted us to their care, and they responded with every kindness. In itself this would have been enough to account for anyone's loyalty to the Faith.

The school system slotted straight on to my grandmother's hierarchy. The main differences were that meaningful spaces and times were enormously multiplied, and rules that had been implicit became explicit. An unexpected consequence was that on being articulated their ambiguities and contradictions were exposed, and begged to be exploited. For example, a rule against running in the corridors (to protect the safety of other users) was supplemented by a rule forbidding talking in the corridors (to keep down the noise level). This irksome rule could be circumvented by grabbing the person you wanted to talk with, and backing together into a doorway. The pleasures of casuistry dawned on us. We lost our innocence about rules, we discovered their facticity and their scope for interpretation: a doorway is not a corridor.

All the times of the day were announced by bells, rung by children designated for that responsible role. Formality distinguished degrees of respect, shown in clothing. We curtseyed to Reverend Mother if we met her unexpectedly. Respect was color coded: if we called on Reverend Mother by appointment we wore our brown gloves, which we also wore for going to chapel, or attending a class in religious doctrine. On holy days we changed our dark uniforms for white, and white gloves, of course. Like my grandmother's house, it was a dual hierarchy. Reverend Mother got this deep respect as head of the whole system; the headmistress, called the Mistress General, came second, but she was actually supreme in everything relating to the school. Normally the nuns would never reprove or humiliate each other in public. But once we saw it happen. The Mistress General found us in the refectory; evidently it was the wrong place and the wrong time. In fury she ticked off the trembling young nun who had shepherded us in there—rebuked her roundly, in front of the school! We were deeply shocked, and indignant.

It was not a competitive environment. The Head Girl was chosen by the nuns (no question of voting) among those who most faithfully kept the rules, not the most popular, or the best scholar, still less the best at games. There was strong moral pressure against signs of personal vanity, against "showing off." If a child really excelled in schoolwork, she would have to be discreet about it. She would not want to be condemned as "brainy." We did play competitive games, hockey and netball in the winter, tennis and cricket in the summer, but not too seriously. A game was more like a choreographed performance. As for showing any satisfaction in winning, that was as disapproved as being a bad loser. I still feel shocked when cricketers or footballers appear on television, the winners openly rejoicing at the downfall of their opponents. We only played matches against other Sacred Heart Schools, who followed the same conventions.

Spatial boundaries were loaded with significance. The nuns lived in an inaccessible area called "Community." Outdoors too, the gardens were large, but the children could only go into specified areas. On holidays, to our great joy, we had privileged access to the school farm and a paddock-like field called "the South of France." The nuns were very formal in their public relations with each other. They had good reason to be reticent about their life in community: I learned some forty years later that in private they enacted the other parts of hierarchy, with moving little ceremonies in which the most senior nuns showed love and respect to the most junior novices. Incidentally, we never saw a nun eat a morsel of food—it was completely forbidden—and we used to tease them by trying to tempt them with delicious chocolates.

A typically hierarchical principle reversed the ranking of the Choir nuns and the Lay Sisters. Choir nuns were educated, most of them had Oxford degrees, and they brought an endowment with them when they entered, called a "dowry." The Lay Sisters had neither dowry nor education, and the religious vows they took were less binding. They didn't sing matins and evensong in choir. Theirs was the rough and necessary menial work that kept the place going. But when it came to reputation for holiness, the Lay Sisters were streets ahead of the Choir nuns. The children eagerly sought their prayers for success in exams and for victories on the hockey field.

Sex was never mentioned. Strict rules governed our bodies. We were never seen even half-naked. We learned ingenious ways of stripping off and changing our clothes without uncovering. In Antonia White's book we read that in my mother's generation the little girls had to wear a long bathrobe in the bath, literally. We used to laugh about it, supposing that it was to prevent us from having impure thoughts if we saw our own nakedness, and not suspecting that the rule was to protect the nun in charge of the bathroom from temptation by the sight of our tender young bodies. My husband tells me that a parallel rule in the Jesuit boys' school was implemented by extraordinarily elaborate plumbing which allowed the priest in charge to regulate the taps from a central point without ever going into a bathroom: "More hot water in No. 7 please Father!"

Some of us benefited from all this rule-driven organization by leaving school as young rebels, resistant to the claims of hierarchy, free to think our own thoughts. Others simply accepted the system, and some, like myself, were endowed thereby with a lifetime project—to make sense of it. For those of us who accepted the system, it made for a happy, sheltered adolescence. But I left school utterly unready for the hurly-burly of real life. And the unreadiness was intensifed on the educational side. The nuns were highly qualified, but they despised "the world." They disdained to worry about bringing the educational standards of the school beyond the requirements for passing the school-leaving certificate. Most of us passed all right, but none of us went to university—until my year when, thanks to a group of specially gifted teachers, four of us went up to Oxford together.[4]

The teaching was good in music, literature, and history. It was not bad in geography, but poor in mathematics, science, and languages. Not surprisingly, it was especially good in history—every year we started again with the Tudors and covered the Reformation with gusto. They taught us to deplore the Protestant secession from Rome and to look down on the Anglican church. The Catholic bishops set up a certificate in Catholic Social Teaching, based on the papal encyclicals *Rerum Novarum* and *Quadragesimo Anno*. I loved those lessons, and wanted to pursue further the questions about social justice, the difference between the living wage and the just wage.

THEOLOGY

Theology was our best subject, it was the nuns' passion, but the School Board did not examine it—a pity, we would have gone through with flying colors. Every day we would put on our brown gloves, leave our normal classrooms and sit in the great hall in a little semicircle of chairs around the teacher. We loved this class, inspired by the enthusiasm of our teachers. The God they talked about was kind and loving. (We were quite surprised when we heard a Passionist Father give a retreat on hellfire). According to our doctrine lessons, God was reasonable and forgiving, and religion was practicable.

Religion was nothing if not transcendental. When we were puzzled, as well we might be, about the Resurrection of the body, the Trinity, the Eucharist, the nuns would whip out the idea of mystery. So we got used to attributing apparent inconsistencies and even contradictions to the inherently weak powers of human understanding. How could our finite human brains encompass the design in the infinite mind of God? This led to discussions of faith, a free gift of God, and our need for the guidance of the Church inspired by the Holy Spirit. Especially dear to the nuns were the numerological mysteries: the Trinity is three persons in one, Jesus is two natures in one, Christ and the Father are two *and* one. What we absorbed well was the idea of a sacramental universe, the capacity of material things to be blessed, the union of Christ's godhead with human flesh as the greatest mystery for which our martyrs had died. The communion of saints was a wonderful cosmic exchange system across the spheres of the living and dead in which anyone might gain profit from the merits of others, and no one could suffer because of others' sins.

There was no danger of blandness. We had a lot of church history, sharpening our minds on how the famous heresies had gone astray. A certain adversarial quality endowed us with self-righteousness—not going so far as to believe that only Catholics went to heaven, but not far off. There was also a confident feminist bias. Clever, good, and dedicated, the nuns believed in womanhood as a divinely given privilege, and paid special devotion to the Blessed Virgin. Women, we learned, were more spiritual, deeper in religious understanding, blessed in being able to bring forth, holy in virginity or in maternity. We were frankly a superior creation, men by comparison were coarse, lusty, and materialist . . . no doubt about it. They had the dignity of priesthood, we had the dignity of womanhood. This assessment of our estate must surely have contributed a sense of intellectual independence when we were later to be launched in a man's world.

FIVE MORE PRINCIPLES OF HIERARCHY

1. The final balance is achieved by dividing the whole system at every level into counterpoised halves, which have their own distinctive spaces, and are expected to compete collectively, within defined limits. (This is the famous historical separation and mutual dependence of the medieval church and state, and the American constitutional separation of powers.)

2. Complementarity is created and imposed by balancing one half against another, at every level, and in carnivals it is shown up by regular ritual reversals.

3. A social hierarchy is like hierarchy in a mathematical sense; it is a rational organization. It uses intellectual justification worked out by equivalencies and analogies.

4. Every situation at every level is judged and justified by reference to analogies, the body is the stock example of corporate unity, and gender the favorite example of complementarity.

5. The final justification is by reference to a comprehensive, universalizing microcosm (the kingdom of God in this case).

A good test of hierarchy is the strength of the bottom-up line of communication. If that is weak the system will tend to become a tyranny ruled from above, and subject to the despot's whims. The balancing of two halves fends off that danger.

UNIVERSITY

So there I was, confident, loyal, rebarbative in defense of my faith, but utterly unprepared for university. Arrived at Oxford I found to my chagrin that exams and hard work were necessary. It put me in some discomfort not to be able to understand the lectures, still less do the maths or statistics. I was not qualified to justify either my good opinion of myself or my loyalties. I had chosen PPE (explained below) because it promised to lead into the social questions raised in the Certificate in Catholic Social Teaching. P stood for philosophy, which at that time, to my dismay, entailed symbolic logic. The second P was for Politics, a relatively soft option, but it entailed a lot of solid library work, and E, for economics, which was just beginning to move heavily into mathematics. It was not a happy time either, as Oxford in wartime was running chaotically on half engines. In 1942, having achieved an undistinguished degree, I was mobilized for war service and directed into the Colonial Office, where I stayed until 1946. I felt very lost, but the good side was that I met anthropologists, read their books, and decided that that was what I really wanted to do. For me there was always going to be an internal dialogue between religion and anthropology, the one illuminating the other, reciprocally.

GRADUATE SCHOOL

After the war I went back to Oxford for graduate study in anthropology, supported by the English equivalent of a "Veterans" grant. It was just as well that Evans-Pritchard had just taken the Chair of Social Anthropology in 1946, as he was a Catholic. In the Colonial Office I had been irritated by anthropologists' quips: "No anthropologist can be a sincere Catholic." In fact the Institute of Anthropology was going to be criticized in years to come for having so many Catholics on its staff. At first it was very cosmopolitan, relatively few English among students and staff: Peristiany was Greek; Srinivas, Indian; Frank Steiner, Jewish; Issa, Egyptian Muslim; Meyer Fortes, South African Jewish. They all took religion very seriously. It was normal to have a religion. I relaxed, for the first time since leaving school, and learned to enjoy hard work for the first time ever.

I did not meet any anti-Catholic prejudice in Oxford. But Evans-Pritchard used to tell a story about Cambridge. Hutton was retiring from his Cambridge chair in anthropology, and Evans-Pritchard and Penniman (curator of the Pitt-Rivers Museum), were among the electors for his successor. Evans-Pritchard was determined to promote Meyer Fortes into that chair, and he prevailed on Penniman to back him. They asked Hutton whether he would be happy to be succeeded by Fortes.

"No, definitely not, he is a Jew."

They then suggested Audrey Richards.

"No, she is a woman. No Catholics, no Jews, no women," said Hutton emphatically.

"Who would you choose, then?" they asked him, and he named Fuhrer Haimendorf.

"But Haimendorf is a Catholic," they demurred.

"Yes, but he is Austrian, that doesn't count, it is just part of his cultural heritage."

Apart from this legend I never heard anything anti-Catholic.

The first book I read in the anthropology introductory course was Evans-Pritchard's *Witchcraft, Oracles and Magic among the Azande.* This study showed, for the first time, that witchcraft accusations did not fall randomly but were structured. Chiefs were not accused by commoners (wisely, as they would have made life difficult for their accusers). Chiefs did not accuse each other, because of a theory that witchcraft was inherited in the male line, so they would be implicating themselves. Women were not accused for another reason. In short, one theory and another narrowed the scope, and the normal pattern was for accusations to cluster in relations that were not buffered by social distance. In other words, people would accuse rivals or enemies who stood in ambiguous or confused relations with themselves and anyone they felt might have reason to dislike or resent them. Belief in witchcraft clarified behavior and intentions.

"Unbuffered"—this suggested that the buffers which hierarchy used to separate people and places had a positive value. Forbidden words and spaces were not just absurd formalities but actually prevented people from offending each other, and actually helped to keep the peace. Or, to put it differently, the rules of hierarchy are rituals of separation—the rules give their symbolic load to spaces and times. Hitherto I had known this intuitively, but had never heard it articulated. A feeling for hierarchy began to be transformed into a feeling for system! I was also reading Durkheim for the first time, and this idea of society as a system of buffered spaces made his teaching congenial to me.

DURKHEIM

Durkheim caused scandal among Christians by teaching that religion is a projection of society: God is called in to ratify the form of society by punishing major breaches of the moral code, and crimes against society are automatically assimilated to crimes against God. It may not strike everyone that it was odd for a Catholic hierarchical upbringing to encourage intuitive sympathy for Durkheimian teaching. But I could never see why the idea of religion as a projection of the social organization was repugnant to Catholics.

Durkheim was bound to attract hostility of pious Christians by announcing his sociological theory of religion from an atheist platform. His general approach went past mythology to concentrate on actions, rituals, 'works,' as distinct from 'faith' and inner experience. It is very much a Catholic principle to relate religion to material existence, so it need not have been seen as anti-Christian to explain changes in religion by social influences and practical issues. Durkheim reversed the whole trend, from academic idealism to pragmatism. It may have sounded reductionist, but it didn't have to be.

I suppose that the nuns had never heard of him; their reading was very controlled. If they had, we would have expected them to back Durkheim against a spiritualizing trend that watered down the full, bold doctrine of the Incarnation as they taught it to us. They had warned us of the heresies against which Augustine had fulminated, the division between spirit and flesh. They taught us to think of religion as a total way of life, robustly material as well as robustly spiritual. Durkheim's sociological view chimed with important distinctions between white and brown gloves, places for talking and places for silence, honor for material things, food, sex, procreation, flesh, blood. Durkheim opened a path into the mysterious unities that religion evokes. I felt that Durkheim was much misunderstood and that it should be possible to sanitize his ideas and make anthropology safe for Catholics.

By the 1960s I had left Oxford and was teaching in London University. But Oxford anthropology had given me an abiding interest in the diversity of culture, always inviting the old question about why religions vary. How do the social systems that uphold the beliefs vary?

How are some hierarchical and others egalitarian? It had been explicit that religion upholds the social system of the believers, and therefore implicit that a new social movement would need to attack the beliefs of the period it was superseding. We certainly should have been ready for the anti-ritualism of the 1960s. But many of us were taken by surprise.

THE LELE OF THE KASAI

In 1949 I went to live among the Lele in the Kasai, in the then Belgian Congo, in order to do fieldwork for my D.Phil. Handsome, clever, imaginative, fun-loving, they were skilled craftsmen in wood and textiles. It was by studying their food taboos and rules about who could enter the forest, the abode of spirits, and at what times, that I started to think about the themes of purity and danger. Certain forest animals were associated with women, and either could not for that reason be eaten by women, or had to be reserved exclusively for women. Carnivores were sorcerers in disguise, and only certain cult initiates could safely eat them. Burrowing animals were associated with the buried ancestors whose underground habitations they shared; birds and squirrels, with God in the sky; fish, with water and fertility spirits. And so on. It was not a matter of taking one taboo at a time, and trying to understand it by itself, it was always a matter of the general pattern. Their cosmology projected the whole of their society onto designated spaces and times, using the technique of prohibitions with which I was very familiar.[5]

I have subsequently come to regard taboos as hierarchizing devices for protecting harmony in thought and order in society. But I did not see it like that at the time because the Lele were not "hierarchical" in any conventional way; on the contrary, they were fanatically egalitarian. They never accepted authority, questioning any attempt to exert it. So the Village Chief was like a constitutional monarch, ceremonial only, with no functions. To make sure he would be useless, the rule was that he had to be the oldest man in the village, so bowlegged, toothless, leaning on a stick. The man who really ran the village affairs was the Village Diviner. He was to the Village Chief as the Mistress

General was to the Reverend Mother at school, or as the wife to the husband in my grandmother's home. And in a typical analogical twist that emphasized their complementarity, the Lele man who held the more effective post bore the title of "Wife-of-the-Village."

Lele had no hierarchies of command except within the family between brothers where seniority by age gave some responsibilities and claims. Instead of an up-down vertical dimension the village structure was based on alternations of status. It was divided in half—the men built their huts in order of age, but alternating the named age groups. The oldest married men, approximately from the age of fifty-plus, lived with their wives and children together at one end, and next to them were the huts of the younger middle-aged men of thirty to forty years. The men of the second oldest age were on the other side; the men from forty to fifty years, next to whom lived the youngest married men, from twenty to thirty. Unmarried men lived together on the outskirts. By this system, age groups adjacent in age were kept apart. The elders on each side were expected to protect and speak for the juniors living with them. A peculiar system, it was intelligible to them as alternation between the generations was a common pattern used in other contexts. Men were allowed to be on intimate personal terms with grandsons, but taboos of mutual respect formally separated them from their sons. The same pattern was carried out in eating rules, sex rules, nakedness rules and speech rules.

What first struck me when I arrived was the absence of authority. No one could get any one else to do anything he didn't want to do. It was very hard to mobilize a working party for anything except hunting. Seeing them again in the perspective of this lecture, and in the perspective of my grandmother's house and the convents, I have to recognize that their taboos and separations were techniques for dispersing power. This is what hierarchy does. For their refusal of authority they paid a big price in lack of coordination. Instead of authority they instituted a heavy encrustation of taboos as buffers separating individuals from others with whom they might be tempted to quarrel. Sadly, this did not entirely prevent feuds and disputes.

If I had been there twenty years earlier, before the last ambush of a district officer in the 1930s, I might have seen a hierarchy that worked. They had still kept the trappings, the separations of places and times, the projection of society on nature, and especially on the wild animals, so that disasters could be plausibly attributed to breach of the rules. But when I was there they had been suffering the gross change of status from free men to colonial subjects. They, who resisted one of themselves giving orders, now themselves had to obey outsiders. Essential parts of their system for living together were not working. Their society was in ruins, and their religion too; fears of sorcery were unchecked, hierarchy was a pious dream in face of the administration, the missions, taxes, labor, and commerce. For the rest of my life, I have been trying to understand this experience.

UNIVERSITY COLLEGE

I stayed in the anthropology department of University College London from 1951 until 1977. It is a wonderful place, founded on liberal principles with the special intention of breaking the hold of the Established Church of England on the universities. Its constitution ruled that no one should be debarred from learning or teaching on account of religious dissent. So Muslims, nonconformists, freethinkers, and Catholics were free to work there. And here we go again! Wanting to make a space for free thought, they created a taboo-like prohibition: there was never to be a divinity school. It became known as the Godless University.

It used to be a very hierarchical structure, authority delegated at every level, and the up-down command structure was matched by strong down-up communications. Responsibility was clear and claims for redress of wrongs could travel easily upwards, from student to head of department, to dean, to provost. I saw it happen and credited this aspect of the system with the much easier time we had in the student riots of 1968 than the egalitarian London School of Economics.

In spite of all the legislation for tolerance, I could not but know that it was odd to be a practicing Catholic (except in the departments of Italian and medieval history). As Noel Annan has described it, the mainstream was rationalist and radical. So I did occasionally hear those old quips. Affectionately enough, Daryll Forde used to tease me:

"How can you bear the hypocrisy of being a Catholic?" A biologist with whom I made friends, when she heard I was a Catholic, exclaimed in astonishment: "In these days! In this college! To hear a thing like that! It makes your mouth go dry!" Trained to nonconfrontation, I held my peace, but privately dismissed such comments as superficial.

The slightly critical atmosphere did me nothing but good. Everyone has to learn to think past the barrier of prejudice. The nuns' pride in intellectual independence was a good support.

PURITY AND DANGER

As I learned about other religions, I came to expect that a religion suited the life of its worshippers, that the beliefs would be adjusted to the circumstances, that if there was to be a reason for local variation it was not even slightly cynical to look for the explanation in the costs and rewards of their way of life, and then to expect worshippers unscrupulously to use their particular heritage of sacred books and signs to promote their struggles with each other, often on quite secular issues. To expect them to find spiritual beings who defend them and attack their enemies, and to call in the cosmos to control each other, blaming the rigors of drought or floods on each others' sins. Seeing how religion gets put to private use prepares one for finding the face of God battered about and transformed in this way or that by religious people. The encounter with Durkheim's approach, and its elegant exposition in the fieldwork monographs of 1950s anthropologists, helped me to shrug off the quips about not being able to be an anthropologist and a Catholic.

My further riposte against the then current anthropology of religion was to write a book about dirt and cleanliness. The main intention of *Purity and Danger*[6] was to join up certain threads that should never have been broken. The cut that had separated us, moderns, from primitives (as we were still allowed to call those others in those days) had to be repaired. Another cut wrongly separated religious speculations in metaphysics and theology from the daily lives and practice of the worshippers. Because of my youthful experience of hierarchy as a system of marked places, and the training that focused on being in the right place at the right time, I was powerfully struck by Lord Chesterfield's definition of dirt as "matter out of place." It provided a rubric that included simple household rules of tidiness and cleaning, and every other kind of patterned separation and arrangement.

We had lived in highly classified worlds, as my grandmother's house or the convent school, worlds constructed from rules about placement and infringements of placing rules. After reading Durkheim and Mauss on classification, I was confident that worlds constructed by taboos would be built the same way. This was how I knew it was a mistake to treat taboo and pollution as matters to be found in exotic cultures but not in our own. Like our own taboos on talking about sex and money, I proposed that foreign taboos are rational attempts to control the flow of information and to resist challenge to a precarious view of the world.

The upheavals of the 1960s had forced some of this on our attention. We were asked vociferously to think about the pollution of rivers, the fate of the little snail darter, and meaningless rituals. At the back of these demands to care for the environment was the distress caused by the Vietnam War, which created a lively concern for injustice of all kinds, poverty, race, and gender. New taboos emerged, such as polluting the pure mountain air with cigarette smoking, and old words became newly defined as incorrect. Seeing the play all round us of the very forces we had been reading about in our anthropology classes was further incentive to pursue this path of enquiry.

CULTURAL BIAS

In *Purity and Danger* I had argued that social beings have a necessary love of order, and feel universally disquieted by its absence. But here were our friends, sane people, inviting disorder, and rejecting order. In one university, enraged students burned the library catalogs, in several places women threw off their restraining garments and burned them. Obviously the idea of a universal preference for order and control needed to be nuanced. "What about artists?" Basil Bernstein expostulated, "Painters revel in dirt and disorder, they thrive in it, the only point of order they want in their world is on the canvas itself." True, not everyone has a strong natural love of hierarchy!

This forced me to rethink my central thesis comparatively. Thanks largely to Bernstein himself I worked on a four-part model of social organizations, each in contrast with the others, and each supported by its own kind of appropriate religion or cosmology.[7] Still following faithfully the convent teaching that the Incarnation is the central Christian doctrine, I assumed, following Durkheim, that without the relevant supporting classifications and values the material aspects of an organization would not be viable, and, vice versa, without the appropriate organization the cultural values would make no sense. Culture and society are one, as are mind and brain.

The work on this fourfold model soon became a tremendously satisfying collective effort.[8] And it still is. Supported by major research of colleagues who have been working on these problems, I have been privileged to take part in a large, developing program to address the initial questions about cultural diversity. I had originally set up a scheme displaying four different kinds of culture, each adjusted to its organizational base.

1. The first of the four cultures we have noted already at length: hierarchy is based on strongly prescribed vertical and lateral boundaries.

2. The next, individualism, is strongly based on competition, not prescription, which makes it weak on boundaries. Its principles are quite incompatible with hierarchy, but a society that can help both cultures to accommodate their aims in agonistic tension is very resilient.

3. Third, enclaves are usually splinter groups that have hived off the mainstream and tend to be egalitarian in principle. This makes them relatively unstructured except for a strong focus on the outside boundary that separates them from the rest of the world. Their rationality is concerned with the ideal just society and protest against an unjust present. The mainstream, based on the mutually antagonistic control of hierarchy and individualism, is well advised to attend to the more sensitive conscience of the enclaves in its midst.

4. The fourth is the culture of the isolates; they tend to belong to categories which are not strongly integrated into the community, often victims of policies designed to satisfy effective lobbies, and often their plight supplies the enclaves with ammunition against the unrighteousness of the other cultures.

This work of categorizing types of organization with each their own appropriate and supporting culture was feeding my longtime interest in religion. Studying their interactions seemed a good way of trying to understand the encompassing role of hierarchy, and how its failure comes about, or could be prevented. This much I understood, but I was stuck with a static model, a mere description of cultural variety, according to which cultural change could only come from outside. I plugged on, examining details of the four particular cultures, but when it came to explaining cultural change, I had to be content with arm-waving toward external factors (like war or new economic opportunity), that could force reorganization entailing the consequent cultural shift. It was a scheme, but not a model because it had no principle of change. Fortunately, and to my great satisfaction, colleagues Michael Thompson and Aaron Wildavsky, twenty years later, dynamized it by recognizing that relations between the said four cultural types are inherently adversarial.[9] This makes it all a lot more interesting. By this means the original method of studying cultural bias was transformed into a theory of political cultures. Over the last twenty years it has produced much interesting theoretical and applied research.

It may be interesting at this point (though out of chronological order), to describe recent developments of Cultural Theory. According to the model of Michael Thompson and other colleagues in policy analysis, any community needs to represent all four cultural types, one hierarchical, one individualist, one enclavist (or protesting sectarian), and a mass of isolates. Each culture keeps the others alive by continuous criticism. At the same time, they must be in conflict because they need the same resources for completely different uses. For example, the uses of time and space in hierarchy shows its incompatibility with individualism, which is more interested in efficient uses of time/space than in celebrating social distinctions. They must inevitably be at odds. The four cultures ought to be in balance; a community in which a high proportion of the population is marginalized would not be able to function democratically, and a community in which the hierarchical principle is very suppressed is in danger of being tyrannized.

The intercultural conflict is good, not bad.[10] If one of the constituent cultures in a community begins to dominate so much as to silence the others, the community will suffer. If this is right, it would apply to the body of Christian churches, and within the Catholic Church, and within any of its communities. The same applies to its relation with the other denominations. In these days, when the concept of hierarchy is so little understood, there is a danger that the unique vocation of a hierarchical church may be forgotten, which would certainly be a loss to the Christian community.

FOOD PATTERNS

In 1977 I retired from University College and joined the staff of the Russell Sage Foundation in New York where my friend Aaron Wildavsky had just become president. Invited to head up a program of research on culture, I chose to limit it to studying food as an object of cultural patterning. The underlying idea was to make a contribution to the methods of studying culture. A group of anthropologists would work together to study the way that food responds to social categories. The idea is deceptively simple, and once again derived from my childhood.

Just as space had been a clear marker of social distinctions in my grandmother's home, so was food, but much more flexibly and concisely primed for marking the calendar. You knew it was Thursday because you saw grilled liver on the dinner table; on Sunday you expected a roast, on Monday cold meat and salad; if it was lunchtime you would expect potatoes, but not if it was tea time. It puzzled me that anyone should spontaneously go to the trouble of making a highly structured meal. Would it not be more normal to be unstructured? What does "highly structured" mean anyway?

We expected that the household in which a lot of social information could be read off the menu would turn out to be more hierarchical than the one in which there is less pattern. Jonathan Gross, in the departments of mathematics and statistics at Columbia University, using information theory and the idea of logical complexity, designed a program of research for us.[11] It showed up the changes over a year in the complexity of menu ingredients according to the changes in the calendar and the guest list. It showed how to trace the breakdown of cultural coherence following migration and other social changes. It also showed that cultural complexity has nothing to do with wealth, and a lot to do with status. Most important, our research provided a measure of social integration. I doubt if this fertile idea has been further exploited.

POWER

When we had barely started this project our president, Aaron Wildavsky, who had hired nearly all of the staff, was unceremoniously fired. His dismissal after only a few months in office gave me poignant and firsthand experience of the culture of large corporations. Though they are commonly taken to be prime examples of hierarchy, their principles and practice fall plumb in the individualist sector of our model of cultural types. In a hierarchy no one can be gratuitously dismissed; in most cases office is held for an agreed fixed term or for life. This gave me more food for thought about the contrast between hierarchy and the culture of individualism.

A hierarchy installs countervailing powers: the husband balanced by the wife, the lord by the bishop, emperor's secular power balancing pope's spiritual authority; registrar and matron facing each other in the hospital. A big school may have two or more heads of houses who can combine to confront the headmaster. Industrial units may have the general manager balanced by the project manager. But the Russell Sage Foundation turned out at that period to be monolithic and arbitrary.

To make up, they gave Aaron Wildavsky what he called "a Presidential ," I used to take the elevator from the thirty-first floor down to his den in the basement (crude spatial symbolism), and we started to work together on risk, and did continue until his untimely death in 1993.

RISK

The cultural theory of risk perception[12] which we launched depends directly on two Durkheimian insights. One was that we should not look to individual psychology for explaining the distribution of blame, but to collective bias ("social representations"). The other was how cultural bias mobilizes political forces. That is, we should study the distribution of political attitudes to the blame-attracting categories: study cultural bias, not private fear and phobia. Like broken taboos, the way that blame falls intensifies the current social conflicts.

The political movement of the 1960s was a forerunner of the revolts against globalism today. A whole generation of generous young people was fired by anger against injustice. By the mid- to late '70s they were forming enclaves and demonstrating against nuclear and other risks that could be laid to the door of industry and government. Aaron Wildavsky was concerned because he was of the generation that in the 1950s had hoped for beneficial economic development and a happier world to be created through nuclear energy. His fellow political scientists were wondering how to explain the shift of values. Why have our values and attitudes changed? They were content to say: "Because there has been a cultural change." It was tautological.

Meanwhile, a new academic industry of risk analysts was moving in whose psychological theories did not explain it any better. So Aaron was attracted to a method of analyzing culture that linked values and beliefs tightly to organizational forms. We went a long way round the current problems in order to start building the political model called "Cultural Theory" that I have referred to above. We were ready now to generalize the typology of cultures I had sketched in 1970 so that it could be applied to modern society.

This time I was only going back as far as Oxford and Evans-Pritchard's 1937 account of witch beliefs in the Sudan, and to Durkheim on public outrage against crime. One question was why certain risks were blown up to catastrophic proportions, while others with a higher and nearer probability of fatality (risks of road accidents, skiing, or sunburn, accidents in the home), were ignored. Crudely, people who are already angry about politics will select risks that can embarrass a political opponent. The other question was why certain categories of persons are preselected to be blamed for the misfortunes that befall.

I admit that the work in this period had little to do with religion. But it had a lot to do with hierarchy. We worked out ways of comparing risk perception in each of the four cultural types, expecting hierarchy to take the longer view and to be less sensitive to personal risks and more sensitive to risks that threatened the whole system. In the 1970s to 1980s the blame was falling along the lines of major social and political conflicts.

I hardly need to say that this approach was not well received by the anti-risk lobbies, or by the categories of business, industry, or government that were their targets. The first did not want to impugn their objectivity, nor the second to admit their own unpopularity. One outcome was to make me aware of blind spots and political bias in parts of the social sciences which are expected to be open-minded and objective about themselves. Which led to several little attacks I have been making against methods of enquiry which would do so much better if they took account of culture instead of trying to theorize about imaginary solipsist individuals.[13]

THE BIBLE

When I left the Russell Sage Foundation, I was glad to be invited to Northwestern University in 1981. To be given a place in the department of the history and literature of religions ought to have been a kind of "coming home," since I had always been interested in religion, and had done so little about it previously. From there I went part time to the religion department in Princeton. Unfortunately, an opportunity was missed in both places. In those years I was still writing on risk and secular institutions instead of working on a topic that would have linked up with my colleagues' researches on religion.

Eventually an invitation from the Presbyterian Seminary at Princeton turned me round. I had been asked as an anthropologist to talk to the students about rituals of sacrifice in the Book of Numbers. It was an eye-opener. I had never read Numbers, but once I started the real homecoming began. Full circle, I was back to the sacred spaces of the convent and the reticences of my grandmother's house—and cleanings, washings, different garments for different places, sins, and a forgiving God.

Numbers is a marvelous and difficult book. It challenged me to go back to the comparison of cultures. The early chapters of my book on Numbers[14] attempt to allocate different religious practices to each of the four cultural types we had used for thinking about risk. Hierarchists would be expected to think of sin and forgiveness differently, more forgiving than enclavist sectarians, more sacramental than individualists. Hierarchists would be more formal and ritualistic. When it comes to celebration, hierarchical religions would celebrate calendrically fixed feasts, while individualists would want to celebrate immediate and local heroic events. Enclavists would be more interested in purity of motive and purity of person, and more concerned to keep up a high boundary against outsiders.

I suggested that the priestly editors were old-style hierarchists. As such they would teach a more assimilationist and open religious doctrine than the xenophobic interpretations of their books that followed the destruction of the second temple. As I read it, the book of Numbers carried a strong political message against Judah's appropriation of the Books of Moses, and against the exclusion of the other sons of Jacob (counted three times over) from their inheritance. Its teaching is to reconcile estranged brothers.

When I went on later, after retiring to England in 1988, to apply the same anthropological critique to Leviticus,[15] my original impression was strengthened. The accepted readings emphasize uncleanness laws and play down God's compassion and forgiveness. Anti-priestly bias could have led later interpreters of the two priestly books to expect careless editing with needless repetition, as I have recorded in my book on Numbers. Leviticus's hierarchical love of complex analogies, its microcosmic analogy of the body and the universe, could escape the attention of enclavist or individualist readers, antique or modern. So when I came to read it as respectfully as an anthropologist would take notes of field observations, I was astonished by the elegance and high style, the superb literary skills, and by the unexpectedly benign theology of love and atonement which for me is the dominant message of

Leviticus. But by now I have made it obvious that I have made not so much an anthropological reading as a reading by a Catholic anthropologist.[16]

CONCLUSION

I should return to the original remit and address the set topic directly. Instead I will try to say why that is impossible. It is because the religious setting of my life has been too pervasive and diffuse. This talk has been very discursive, but it had to be like this. It had to be about places, corridors, bathrooms, food, clothes, and gloves, because the theme is another of the body/soul, spirit/matter, mind/brain mysteries which the nuns gave up trying to explain in words, but which as schoolchildren we learned by objects and actions. The interaction between religion as I was taught it and anthropology as I discovered it has been too continuous and intimate to be disentangled. All I can say is that for me there was always going to be an internal dialogue between religion and anthropology, each illuminating the other. There it is.

CHAPTER 8

My Life as a "Woman": Editing the World

MARGARET O'BRIEN STEINFELS

A VERY BRIEF HISTORY OF RECENT TIMES

The history of our time is a history of change, really of revolutionary change. Revolutions in the sciences, in weaponry, in international relations, in agriculture, in cooking, in relations between men and women, in gender identity, in child rearing. The essential measures of our earthly existence, time and space, we understand in far more complex ways that we did even twenty years ago. Furthermore, all such changes themselves become the springboard for ever greater change, what the British sociologist Anthony Giddens calls "institutional reflexivity." By that he means "the regularized use of knowledge about circumstances of social life as a constitutive element in its organization and transformation."[1] By this definition, it is not true that the more we change the more we stay the same. No, the more we change the more we are subject to further change.

Not only do we live through change, in a matter of five years change becomes the stuff of history, and in ten years the stuff of revisionist history (consider the collapse of the Soviet Union in 1990, and the variety of theories we now entertain about its cause or causes), to say nothing of political science, sociology, psychology, and biology. The business of such scholarship and academic specialization is generalization that spills over into theory making. This in turn spills over into more popular generalizing in the science section of the *New York Times*, diet books, op-ed pieces on United States foreign policy, books on self-help or child nutrition (fifty years ago many American children suffered severe forms of malnutrition; now, they suffer from obesity). And, that quintessential American research tool, the opinion poll, speeds up the pace of change ever more rapidly.

It is true that human beings offer various forms of resistance to this modern propensity for revolutionary change. We are too lazy, too critical, too busy, too skeptical; we don't answer opinion polls, we don't watch television and have stopped reading the newspaper. Still, we all recognize that individual lives are, willy-nilly, affected by these changes. Sometimes those lives become major players in revolutionary change (Catholics, whether in favor or opposed, have had to respond to the changes brought on by Vatican II). Sometimes individuals are caught up in revolutions not of their own making (the family farm is almost extinct, and with it millions of jobs; blue-collar jobs are fast disappearing into cheaper labor markets; high school educations no longer prepare young women or men for good jobs). Some people live lives parallel to vast changes and seem to be unaffected by them. (Only contrast our current first lady, Laura Bush, with our previous one, Hillary Rodham Clinton. What is Mrs. Bush's family name?) Sometimes lives are unexpected catalysts for change (My fellow graduates of St. Scholastica High School, 1959, did not expect to be part of a revolution in women's lives, yet here we are). Sometimes lives move counter to the main thrust of change (whether or not the family farm is a relic, the Amish go right on running them). And because revolutions unfold over time, however brief, sometimes many of these possibilities are at play in a given life.

Recently I had to read more than a dozen books on women and Catholicism for a book review. There were personal narratives, scholarly works, efforts at reappropriation (Catherine of Siena and Joan of Arc as feminist models) or theological invention (Mary Magdalene is proposed to be the first apostle). Of course, these volumes are written in light of the revolution in women's lives. And no surprise: it is a precarious business reconceiving history and creating narratives about the vast and multilayered changes that have affected women's lives, in fact, the lives of everyone—men and children as well as women—over the last half century, lives that are still in play. These books that I have been reading have their own conceptual frameworks and often a strongly stated thesis (why, some even have ideological spin). None-theless, I suspect that they diverge from the lived experiences of most women, indeed, perhaps of the author herself or himself.

So my first point: Life is not an ideology or a political agenda or a conceptual framework but a continuing set of relationships and responsibilities that shape our response to revolutionary change. At the end of a day on the barricades everyone still has to go home and eat dinner.

The women's revolution is a complicated matter, having its origins in many sources (recall, for example, that the contraceptive pill was developed by Dr. John Rock, a Catholic doctor, who firmly believed that his pill would meet the strictures of the Catholic sexual ethic), and drawing its strategies from many corners of political thought—anarchist, reformist, sexual liberationist, liberal, and reactionary. Despite this complexity, there is in the United States a uniform, even rigid, narrative about the revolution in women's lives. In its popular form it begins in 1963 with the publication of *The Feminine Mystique* by Betty Friedan—I was given a copy on my twenty-third birthday by the radical feminist Peter Steinfels. Over the years since, this revolution has had its triumphs in equal opportunity laws, successful sexual harassment suits, and women in elected office; its cultural triumph in Title IX funding for women's college athletics, which has resulted in brilliant soccer and basketball teams fielded by women,[2] and in many firsts for women, first Supreme Court justice, first secretary of state, first president of an Ivy League school, first CEO of a Fortune 500 company.

For reasons somewhat accidental to this revolution, state abortion laws in the United States were stricken down in 1973. And despite so many other notable achievements, political and social, that Supreme Court decision has become the talisman of the official woman's move-ment. *Roe v. Wade* is the sole litmus test by which politicians, judges, regulators, businesses, and women themselves are judged to be in favor, or not, of this vast revolution in the lives of all of us; it is the funding standard for Emily's List—the country's largest political ac-tion fund for women. Needless to say, there are other feminist scenarios. Mary Kenny, the Irish journalist, tells a different story about the women's movement in that nation, and about the views of Ireland's woman president (its second woman president!) Mary McAleese; she is pro-life and pro-ordination of women.

Reading these recent books put me in mind of my own trajectory through what can legitimately be called a world historical shift—or at least that's what we call it in our house—of women's lives and prospects. The women's revolution is a world historical shift like the shift from hunting and gathering to settled agricultural life thousands of years ago. Or like the shift in North America and Europe from agricultural to industrial economies, which began in the nineteenth century and continues to this very day in Eastern Europe, Central Asia, Africa, and Latin America. This is a shift that is changing the lives of millions of women in and of itself, quite apart from the women's revolution. Like these earlier revolutions, the women's revolution moves across the world in fits and starts. Unlike these earlier revolutions, the pace is faster, and almost certainly inexorable.

I mention all of this to lay the groundwork for distinguishing among what the books and studies and popular mythology say has happened to women, what each of us says about our self in the midst of this revolution, and what actually has happened, if that can ever be fully determined.

MY LIFE AS A "WOMAN"

What I am about to recount is itself a narrative, one that may seem as elusive or unlikely as the conjecture that Mary Magdalene was the first apostle. Like that story it contains possibly false or forgotten memories (to say nothing of false consciousness), texts are lost or never existed, anecdotes that I often tell about myself are sometimes claimed to be the property of Peter, my husband, or our children. Anthony Giddens has these perceptive words about personal narrative, and I offer them to confirm the skeptical: "The individual's biography, if she is to maintain regular interaction with others in the day-to-day world, cannot be wholly fictive. It must continually integrate events which occur in the external world, and sort them into the ongoing 'story' of the self."

I cannot say that my life as a woman has been of much interest to me or to anyone else. I am not radical—or reactionary—enough. The only "first" on my CV is being *Commonweal*'s first woman editor-in-chief (but not its first woman editor: that was Helen Walker, who was a founding member of the staff in 1924). Being a woman has not been a major subject in my writing, nor does it loom large in my editorializing, or my thinking. In fact, one of the great achievements of the women's movement is that at last women are not limited to writing about women and children. I have been able to write about war and peace, Bosnia, Kosovo, and Iraq, about politics and bioethics, about cloning, about liturgy, clergy, and church politics, about civil rights, international law, and the movies. That doesn't mean I haven't pontificated at the dining room table, or read books on the subject, which occupy several of my bookshelves. And, of course, I recognize that it is only because I am a woman that people sometimes ask me what I think about matters Catholic. Earlier in the summer a reporter asked for an interview about Pope John Paul II's twenty-five years in office. "Why me?" I asked. He hesitated for a nanosecond, and said, "Well, you're a woman." One must have a woman!

In any case, the narrative you are about to hear is one I have constructed partly in light of having had to read all of those books over the last three months. In that short time, this narrative has had different titles. Once it was called "A Life: History Notwithstanding." (That was a takeoff on Hillary Clinton's *Living History*). For a while this narrative was called "The Princess and the Pea" (in recognition of my editorial propensity to get at that one last lump in the prose, just like the princess in Hans Christian Andersen's story who felt the pea under twenty mattresses and eiderdown comforters). But today it's called "My Life as a 'Woman,'" because as I read over those fifteen books, I realized that it had been a long time since I had given much thought to "my life as a woman," and here I was being asked on the occasion of the Marianist Award to speak about my faith and my life, particularly my work.

This narrative is subtitled "Editing the World" because that's what I've been doing all my life, and that is what I am doing as I speak.

This subject like any other certainly requires editing. It will always require editing.

Point two: Great social and cultural changes show up only incrementally in the lives of most individuals. Large-scale ideations, collections of ideas that try to explain the world, whether of Plato, Sigmund Freud, Karl Marx, Karol Wojtyla, Erma Bombeck, Betty Friedan, or Mary Daly are always ambiguous, sometimes useless, in explaining our actual lives. That is, they don't necessarily explain to us what has happened to us. Betty Freidan diagnosed "the problem without a name," a problem for some white, college-educated, middle-class women raising children in the American suburbs of the 1950s.

Karol Wojtyla has used the word *complementarity* to describe the relationship between men and women, even though we see that the distinctive character traits of men and women the theory requires are dispersed over the range of human behavior, whether male or female. At least in modern times, it is nurture and culture more than nature and biology that develop in human persons the qualities they need to flourish. If reproduction once sharply defined the roles and behaviors of men and women, it no longer does, certainly not over a life span of seventy-five to eighty years, and not in the last fifty years.

Point three: For revolutions to take off, there must be people ready for them. American Catholics, perhaps women especially, were more than ready for the revolution in women's lives, in the way we think about women, in the way we think about how the world would work if only we had a say in the running of it. There are a number of reasons for this. Let me offer three.

First, women religious were examples of alternative lives, not because they weren't married, but because they founded, organized, and maintained great institutions and systems. These included parish schools, hospitals, and social service centers; day-care centers, high schools, and colleges (and, as many biographies and institutional histories show, they sometimes built and worked in contest rather than cooperation with the bishop or parish priest). They passed on these traits of independence and enterprise to millions of Catholic boys and girls.

Second, American Catholics were ready for the revolution in women's lives because of social class. There is nothing like an immigrant and/or working-class upbringing in the United States to make men and women energetic and ambitious for themselves and their children (as we see today with immigrants from ever more diverse cultures).

Third, Catholics in the United States, though not complete outsiders to the Protestant culture of the 1940s, '50s, and '60s, had an establishment of their own. The throw weight of Catholics, demographically, politically, and institutionally, was more than sufficient to catapult us forward into the mainstream of American life, women as well as men—a leap commonly symbolized by the election of John F. Kennedy in 1960.

Some examples of Catholic readiness from my family: Paid employment is thought to be a great change in the lives of American women. But I grew up in a family where most of the women always worked outside their homes as well as in them. My mother worked as a bookkeeper and an executive assistant, the kind of office fixer that makes everything work everywhere (no doubt, in this university too), my grandmother was a private-duty nurse, and my aunts were secretaries, office managers, telephone operators, political fixers, the kind that kept Chicago working. They didn't talk about their jobs; they didn't speak of careers. Did they want an existence apart from their families? They never said so. Was staying at home, like Friedan's suburban wives, a luxury that they couldn't afford, or a domestic confinement they didn't want? Like the men, they worked to support their families. Some supported themselves. They all wanted their children to have Catholic educations, and worked to pay for that goal.

I was the first beneficiary in my family of a college education—at Loyola University in Chicago. I was expected to contribute my part by being a good student and having a job. I was a good student and I worked, at part-time jobs from the time I was in seventh grade. This was also educational: I learned something important about both work and money.

At a relatively young age, I was able to make these elementary observations: work was hard, sometimes boring, and for most people work was not an end in itself. Certainly you did not enjoy your work, and if you did, you didn't talk about it. Work might have some side benefits, friendships, improving working conditions, being active in a union, gossiping about the petty claims of authority by idiot bosses (I grew up in a family where bosses were always idiots, their motives always suspect. And having been a boss myself for fifteen years, I can see why they thought that). I also learned that money was important, but not all-important. Having money, making money was not an end in itself (a penny saved was a penny earned); there was such a thing as having enough money. You didn't have to go into law or investment banking to make money or have enough of it.

As a college student, also working part time, I came to the conviction that it would be a good idea to have work that I liked, that was not boring, and not deadening to the human spirit, in other words, a job that involved reading and writing. I think I have succeeded in finding that kind of work, not by pulling myself up by my own bootstraps as the national myth has it, but through the generous tutelage and mentoring of others.

American Catholics stand on the shoulders of giants, many of them women. Because of the Catholic Church everybody in my family was safely delivered at birth, baptized and blest, taught to pray, prepared for First Communion, and given terrific educations and a purpose in life. The Catholic subculture of pre–Vatican II days has come in for its lumps (the 1979 play *Sister Mary Ignatius Explains It All for You*, sexual repression, the 2002 Irish movie *The Magdalene Sisters*, etc.), but the record in my personal archive is overwhelmingly positive. On the other hand, sufficient time has passed that those years have acquired for many people, who mostly weren't there, a deep rich patina of nostalgia, especially about the Latin Mass and the Baltimore Catechism. My experience: Nothing wrong with them, until you have experienced something better.

But the Catholic Church isn't the only institution that suffers dystopian memories. We all know, don't we, that before the women's movement began, on or about 1963, the publication date of *The Feminine Mystique*, women suffered discrimination, even oppression—legal, social, cultural, and political—at the hands of a patriarchal ideology. In their families, preference was given to men, and women spent their lives in kitchen drudgery. The Catholic Church was run by men ergo it was the worst of the lot, along with Catholic families, who had too many children anyway. Everyone forgets the sisters who actually ran most of the Catholic Church. We all talk about the decline in the number of priests; we all lament it. What about the decline in the number of women religious? We all talk about the needs of retired sisters, yet women's religious congregations remain a place where authority and influence still reside in truly gifted women. I think of some of those women: Sister Sharon Euart, Sister Doris Gottemoeller, and the late Sister Margaret Cafferty, women of authority. And add Sister Sandra Schneiders, who is the author of one of those fifteen books I read, *With Oil in Their Lamps*, a fair-minded, intelligent, brief, and comprehensive state of the question about *Faith, Feminism, and the Future*, the book's subtitle.

Point four: When I went to Loyola University, I found that men were my allies, indeed, the allies of any woman student who was serious about studying. Not that I knew what I needed allies for, or what I was going to study. What I did know was that I was in a place where I could read and write and where the life of the mind and a life of action were given fertile soil. I had landed in an agonistic culture, a culture of contest and disputation (I didn't know the word *agon* until some years later, when I read Walter Ong's brilliant book *Fighting for Life*). This was a culture that valued intellectual contest, rhetorical play, the pursuit of ideas, and politics with a small *p*. The Jesuits created an atmosphere geared to the development of little anti-authoritarians of all genders. The university administration was the equivalent of all the bosses my family made fun of for petty authoritarianism. Some of the more imaginative moments in student life involved getting around the rules and thwarting orders from on high (but perhaps that was the pedagogic function of student life—those Jesuits can be clever).

Of course, there were among these men generous teachers and administrators, of whom the distinguished scripture scholar John L. McKenzie, then S.J., was among the most brilliant and idiosyncratic. A Hoosier, he called himself a Taft Republican in a city where no one had ever voted for a Taft and hardly anyone had ever voted for a Republican. In reality, he was a political anarchist who believed the great error of ancient Israel, in the decline of civilization, was installing a monarchy—it has been all downhill since. John McKenzie was one of those scripture scholars silenced in the 1950s by the Vatican, which only increased the dim view of authority that he seems to have been born with. When he was finally allowed to teach at Loyola in 1961, he turned the full force of his brainpower, knowledge, and love of learning on us undergraduates. It was bracing for a twenty-year-old history major (and it was in the history, not theology, department that he taught) to be thrown into layers of text, layers of history, layers of the history of texts, and made to come to grips with the reality of what was for a young Catholic the almost mythological nature of the Hebrew Scriptures, then called the Old Testament.

I will not go on with the male ally theme except to mention my fellow students, Peter Steinfels and Barry Hillenbrand, living examples of the power of contest and ideas, who introduced me to the thrills of student journalism. And to add that later in life Robert Hoyt at the *National Catholic Reporter*, Daniel Callahan at the Hastings Center, Philip Murnion at the National Pastoral Life Center, and James O'Gara at *Commonweal* all gave me the wherewithal and the space to become a writer, editor, and journalist.

But who, you might ask, gave me the chutzpah? When young, I was not as cheeky as I have become (I lived in fear of being caught doing something that was against the rules). A sterling example was set for me in 1963 when two of my classmates, women, decided to test racial equality at the Catholic Women's Club swimming pool, supposedly open to all women university students. African-American Mickey Leaner (then a Negro) was refused an application for admission; Nancy Amidei (then and now a white girl) was not. The two seemed to me exceptionally courageous in trying out this novel tactic of the civil rights movement in Chicago, and exposing the university's own hidden corner of segregation. The student newspaper reported it, of course. And shortly thereafter, nuns, Franciscans I believe, in habit picketed—a first for women in habits.

Point five: Catholics and Catholic women were ready for revolution in women's lives. And if the revolution we are living through isn't exactly the one we want; it is the one we have taken advantage of and the one that, in many respects, has served us well. It is also one that could use some serious Catholic correctives about abortion, about community, and about the permanent responsibility of marital relationships.

But if some American Catholics, women and men, nuns and priests, were ready for the women's revolution, the Catholic Church it turns out was not. On or about October 15, 1976, the Catholic Church shifted from being merely a patriarchal institution of a somewhat absent-minded, even unconscious kind, no worse than most institutions—no worse than Harvard, Harvard Law School, the Democratic Party, the AFL-CIO, the FBI, the Supreme Court of the United States, the United Nations, the French Republic, the National Council of Churches. After all, in the American Catholic Church, women actually had influence and authority; some even had power.

On October 15, 1976, the Catholic Church made itself a sexist institution bent on excluding women from the priesthood and thereby from decision-making and governance responsibilities.

> The Sacred Congregation for the Doctrine of the Faith judges it necessary to recall that the Church, in fidelity to the example of the Lord, does not consider herself authorized to admit women to priestly ordination. . . . It is a position which will perhaps cause pain but whose positive value will become apparent in the long run, since it can be of help in deepening understanding of the respective roles of men and of women. (*Inter insigniores*)

Since then, at its highest levels, the Catholic Church has systematically excluded from episcopal office anyone who publicly advocates the ordination of women. Theologians have been disciplined for raising the question and denied teaching posts in pontifical schools. The pope has frowned at public mention of it.

Well, perhaps the prohibition on ordaining women has been divinely revealed. But then, why all the litmus tests? Is it because the theological claims have failed to convince most Catholics, men and women, nuns and priests, probably even some bishops? Perhaps there are anthropological questions about women's ordination that should give us pause, but then shouldn't these be the subject of vigorous discussion and debate? In fact, most women don't want to be priests—neither do most Catholic men; and at this sad and perplexing moment in our history, most women probably don't want their sons or daughters to be priests either. Certainly I don't expect to see a woman priest on a Catholic altar in my lifetime. Yet once again in 1994 (in *Ordinato sacerdotalis*), Pope John Paul II considered it necessary to repeat the ban and reinforce the claim: "I declare that the church has no authority whatsoever to confer priestly ordination on women and that this judgment is to be definitively held by all the church's faithful." Why has the Vatican felt it necessary to construct what will prove to be a Maginot Line? I think because it has no credible arguments. Despite all of the fine words about the importance of women and the role of women by this pope and other Vatican officials, indeed, in the very documents I just quoted, the Catholic Church at its highest levels fears women (Who me? Who us?). Or so I conclude.

What then to make of the positive and benign narrative I have offered about my own experience as a Catholic and a woman. Well, it is American, and it is generational; it reflects the American Catholic Church of the 1940s, '50s, and '60s in Chicago, which was able to read the signs of the times. It is true that young Catholics today live in a church that has opened doors for women in academia, in chancery offices, in parishes. But no woman in parish, diocesan, or Vatican jobs is welcome in more than an advisory role, and all are barred from decision making or governance of the Catholic Church, and will be for the foreseeable future, since ordination is required. And if women cannot help to govern the church now, even perhaps as papal electors (a job that Jesus did not institute), will that hold true in the lifetime of my children, my grandchildren, great-grandchildren? What a pity! But who would be surprised? Will there be any Catholic women left?

EDITING THE WORLD

Let me conclude with some editorial notes dated August 31, 2003:
This narrative by Margaret O'Brien Steinfels may strike some listeners as Pollyannaish. What about the Sturm und Drang of adoles-

ence, of young motherhood; the Sturm und Drang of learning German? What about the arguments and debates with her mother and father about quitting that college education course, which would have made her a teacher—and given her the security of a civil service job? What if she had interviewed her own children—and her daughter reported the terrible argument they had in or about September 1985 over whether to take a course on the Black Death (a critical turning point in Western history) or Japanese monuments (not a major historical issue, even for the Japanese)? What about all of the arguments she has had with those men she counted as allies, including the one she deeply loves and is married to? And the many more arguments with men who were not her allies? What about her reflexive antipathy to those converts to Catholicism, mostly men, who wage their battles against modernity and against women from the battlements they are constructing around the Catholic Church into which she was so happily born? And what does she really think about ordaining women? Should she have mentioned that the appointment of Madeleine Albright as secretary of state was the occasion for more thought than she is likely to give the ordination of the first woman, which as she says is not likely to happen in her lifetime?

Can the author of this narrative be relied upon?

What kind of woman is she?

Well consider this: whatever kind of woman she turns out to be, she's still a practicing Catholic, and she needs a lot more practice.

As they say on the Fox News Network: We report. You decide.

CHAPTER 9

Liberal Catholicism Reexamined

PETER STEINFELS

I often think it's comical
How Nature always does contrive
That every boy and every gal,
That's born into the world alive,
Is either a little Liberal,
Or else a little Conservative!
                    (*Iolanthe*, act 2)

I was born into the world a liberal Catholic. Exhibit A: My liturgically oriented parents sent out not the standard birth announcement but a card with simple religious symbols and the wording,

> The Lord of life has visited Margaret and Melville Steinfels
> with a child Peter Francis
> born a child of Adam on July 15, 1941
> reborn of water and the Holy Ghost a child of God
> on July 27, 1941.

In 1941, this kind of announcement was enough to cause a stir. One irreverent wag in the family wrote back "Who is this fellow Adam? And does Mel know about him?"

I was born into the world, as I said, a liberal Catholic. Which is to say that, contrary to W. S. Gilbert, I was not *either* a little liberal *or else* a little conservative. I was, and I remain, *both* a little bit liberal *and* a little bit conservative. Nothing better illustrates the Catholic tendency toward both/and instead of either/or than liberal Catholicism.

How can one define liberal Catholicism? One way is that it is what the *Syllabus of Errors* had in mind when, in its famous final salvo, it condemned the idea that "the Roman pontiff can and ought to reconcile and harmonize himself with progress, with liberalism, and with modern civilization."[1]

Another way to define it is that liberal Catholicism is simply papal teaching a hundred years too soon.

Liberal Catholicism is, in fact, a controverted and approximate label. It was applied, often pejoratively, to nineteenth-century figures like Lamennais, Lacordaire, Montalembert, Bishop Dupanloup, and Marc Sangnier in France, to John Henry Newman and Lord Acton in England, to Daniel O'Connell in Ireland, to Isaac Hecker and John Ireland in America, and to a host of other thinkers and leaders in Belgium, Italy, Poland, and Germany. Its history overlaps with that of Christian Democracy, social Catholicism, and modernism.

But it is important to note that liberal Catholicism was rooted in Romanticism more than in the Enlightenment. Its rebellion against the old alliance of throne and altar, and its eventual embrace of freedom of religion for all, was restorationist, not revolutionary: it began not with the Enlightenment's desire to free politics from the stranglehold of priestcraft but to free the church, indeed with the papacy at its head, from bankrupt regimes so that the faith might again conquer society through witness and persuasion rather than coercion.[2]

If those are conservative DNA sequences in liberal Catholicism's genetic constitution, the liberal DNA sequences are perhaps more obvious.

First, liberal Catholicism insisted on discriminating rather than blanket judgments about the French Revolution and the modern liberties and social upheavals the revolution signaled.

Second, liberal Catholicism believed that change and development had become the normal, not the exceptional, state of things, a reality to be embraced as opportunity rather than lamented or denounced as affliction.

Third, liberal Catholicism trusted in the power of truth to prevail if allowed free play on the terrain of free discussion.

Fourth, liberal Catholicism defended the relative autonomy of distinct spheres of human activity, whether of politics or religion or science or art and literature; each field has its independent criteria that must be scrupulously respected, although ultimately the formed conscience must make moral judgments.

Finally, liberal Catholicism, despite its protagonists' piety and papal loyalties, found it impossible to separate its project of evangelizing society from issues of internal church reform.

None of this was taught me in a liberal Catholic version of the Baltimore Catechism. My parents just read *Commonweal* and the *Catholic Worker* and novels by Mauriac and Bernanos. Our bookshelves carried lots of books published by Sheed and Ward, indeed lots of books written by Frank Sheed and Maisie Ward.[3] My father belonged to a generation of artists that hoped to rescue liturgical art from the mass-produced images and statuary of the religious goods companies. The family entertained the idea, then verging on heresy, as I found out when I voiced it at St. Paul of the Cross school, that the Mass ought to be celebrated in the people's own language, as it had been in the early days of the church.

Liberal Catholicism was the air I breathed, matter for my college and graduate studies, and something I guess I later perpetrated at *Commonweal.* Four years ago, I gave a kind of State of the Union address on liberal Catholicism for that magazine's seventy-fifth anniversary. It was published in the November 19, 1999, issue.[4]

I

The genesis of that talk was the claim, advanced in a homily almost two years earlier by Archbishop, soon to be Cardinal, Francis George of Chicago. "Liberal Catholicism is an exhausted project," he said. "Essentially a critique, even a necessary critique at one point in our history, it is now parasitical on a substance that no longer exists. It has shown itself unable to pass on the faith in its integrity and inadequate, therefore, in fostering the joyful self-surrender called for in Christian marriage, in consecrated life, in ordained priesthood. It no longer gives life."

The remedy, he went on, was not to be found in a type of obsessively conservative Catholicism either. "The answer is simply Catholicism, in all its fullness and depth."

It was just Cardinal George's luck that one of the people in the pews that evening was Margaret O'Brien Steinfels. Not the sort to let such remarks float by unnoticed, she raised questions in person and then in print about these characterizations of both liberal Catholicism and "simply Catholicism"—and she invited the cardinal to respond.

Ultimately he very generously did—at a forum, held in Chicago, for that seventy-fifth anniversary. My own analysis, prepared without any exact knowledge of how he would expand on his earlier claims, followed. I did not consider liberal Catholicism at all an exhausted project in the sense of being no longer needed. Quite the contrary. But I did fear it ran the risk of exhaustion, in the sense of being beaten down, thrown into disarray, assailed by forces both secular and religious, on both right and left.

Prominent leaders in Rome and self-declared "orthodox" Catholics in the United States increasingly seemed determined to brand liberal Catholicism disloyal and root it out. In American politics and culture, liberal Catholicism had few friends now that abortion had become the critical litmus test for secular liberalism, and tax cuts, market solutions, and military assertiveness become de rigueur for conservatism. Finally, liberal Catholicism found itself allied, entangled, and sometimes eclipsed in a complicated relationship with what has come to be labeled the Catholic left.

It was to this latter topic that I devoted a large part of my talk. As the Holy Cross historian David O'Brien has explained, in the years after the Second Vatican Council a Catholic left was born out of liberal Catholicism but quite consciously defined itself over against it. "The use of the phrase left," he wrote in the 1999 book called *What's Left?* edited by Mary Jo Weaver, "raises the question: left of what? The Catholic left emerging from the sixties had a ready answer: left of liberal Catholicism."[5]

The line of demarcation, alas, is very blurry. I have suggested that *America* and *Commonweal* stand on the liberal Catholic side of the line, and the left begins with the *National Catholic Reporter* and runs through Pax Christi and Call to Action and Dignity perhaps to Catholics for a Free Choice. Yet one could even trace the boundary between different bylines in the *National Catholic Reporter*! Much academic moral and systematic theology, biblical scholarship, liturgical studies, and catechetics belong in liberal Catholic territory, but not all; and some feminist thought and liberation theology are indisputably to the left.

O'Brien stresses the differing styles of these clusters. Liberal Catholics affirm the positive values of the culture and its democratic institutions; they stress dialogue, mediation, compromise, and gradualism. It is a style more incarnational than countercultural and grounded in the lay experience of work, family, and politics. It is rooted, I would add, in the European church's struggles with liberty, the Enlightenment, totalitarianism, and secularization, all forming the background to Vatican II.

The Catholic left's style, O'Brien says, is more evangelical, perhaps as some would have it more prophetic, or perhaps, as others would say, more sectarian. It measures church, society, and culture starkly against Gospel standards. It is a style rooted in the dramatic appeals and confrontational tactics of the 1960s and more linked to the third-world liberation movement than to nineteenth- and twentieth-century European experiences.

As O'Brien states and the book *What's Left?* amply illustrated, the Catholic left has become largely defined by internal church questions of gender, sexuality, ecclesiology, worship and spirituality, a near rejection of hierarchy, and a consistently political style of lobbying and mobilization organized around the demands of various special constituencies more than any sense of the whole. If one were to name concrete objectives—for example, regarding women in the church, collaborative decision-making, or a rethinking of sexuality—one might conclude that they are broadly shared by this Catholic left and by liberal Catholicism. If one looks to fundamental convictions and attitudes in a larger sense, the gap between the two neighboring camps is far more significant.

For myself, both liberal Catholicism and the Catholic left faced additional problems, each of which I analyzed at some length. One was a lack of irony about unanticipated consequences, indeed a culpable innocence of the modern historical record of idealistic causes bent to tragic and even criminal outcomes. A second was a creeping anti-intellectualism, rooted in the partisan spirit rampant in the church but also rooted in the recognition of experience as material for religious reflection. Certainly on the Catholic left and to a considerable extent within liberal Catholicism, personal experience, witness, and testimony have become the dominant mode of approaching issues. Conversion and sacrifice are in the foreground. Systematic analysis of causes and effects, of underlying principles, of relationships to a web of other evidence, or most importantly to a heritage of theory, doctrine, and wisdom is minimized. Third and finally I proposed that inclusiveness had become a dangerous fetish, inhibiting serious examination of issues of Catholic identity.

These weaknesses afflicted both liberal Catholicism and the Catholic left, I argued, and each camp would have to address them in its own way. That task was made more difficult by the fact that common origins, working alliances, and public perception led the two camps, even in their own eyes, to be practically identified. In practice, I said, many liberal Catholics go their own rather more moderate way, but without challenging this identification or articulating any public criticism of the Catholic left. But could liberal Catholicism maintain this discreet silence? Wouldn't it be obliged, in some cases, not only to engage in self-criticism itself but also to call the Catholic left to account?

My talk was an effort to do both those things and to encourage others to do them as well. No such luck. To say that it stirred even a ripple of response among either liberal or left Catholics would border on exaggeration.

In the end, the most substantial challenges remained Cardinal George's argument that liberal Catholicism was an exhausted project and a more recent critique by Richard John Neuhaus,[6] arguing that liberal Catholicism had not only been led seriously astray by its "dubious allies" on the left but even more fundamentally by its failure to come to terms with the requirement for Catholics of obedience.[7]

II

These are serious arguments. Both, I believe, are badly flawed. Both raise issues, however, that liberal Catholicism can only benefit by confronting.

Cardinal George and Father Neuhaus describe liberal Catholicism in terms similar to mine. For Cardinal George, the liberal Catholic project was a response to the Enlightenment, which he equates with modernity.

"The challenge for the church," he said, "lay in distinguishing the erroneous aspects of modernity from those that were compatible with, and even developments of, the Christian faith." Unfortunately, the trauma of the French Revolution for the church would subject the Enlightenment project to a century of condemnations.

"In the midst of the controversy, a group now known as the 'liberal Catholics' began to distinguish and assess the various aspects of modernity," he noted. These liberal Catholics rejected cultural aspects like materialism, secularism, moral relativism, and individualism, but they urged the adoption of certain political and economic aspects that would equip the church better to redeem the culture. "The church's engagement with the modern world it had both resisted and helped create eventually resulted in the endorsement of a free society found in *Dignitatis Humanae, Gaudium et Spes*, and *Centesimus Annus*."

Father Neuhaus was even more affirming of my description of liberal Catholicism, at least at first glance. If this is liberal Catholicism, he stated, "we should all want to call ourselves liberal Catholics." And then he added, "which is another way of saying that, although Mr. Steinfels and others may have problems with this, we should be John Paul II Catholics."

I cannot speak for others. For me, the problem is not some link between liberal Catholicism and the present pope. As I said, one definition of liberal Catholicism is simply papal teaching a hundred years too soon. For me, the problem is the extraordinary leap, made by Cardinal George and Father Neuhaus alike, over all the painful, even tragic, history in between.

It is well and good to declare that we are all liberal Catholics today. What about being a liberal Catholic in the 1830s, 1850s, or 1890s, when, as I documented in my talk, liberalism was being portrayed by popes and papal champions as "the evil of evils"—"the offspring of Satan"—"a greater sin than blasphemy, theft, adultery, homicide, or any other violation of the law of God." And liberal Catholics were a particularly dangerous "monstrosity"—"less excusable than those liberals who have never been within the pale of the Church."

For Pius IX, liberal Catholicism was "pernicious," "perfidious," "perverse," a "virus." "I have always condemned liberal Catholicism," he told a delegation of French Catholics in 1871, "and I will condemn it again forty times over if it be necessary." "Liberal Catholics are wolves in sheep's clothing," wrote the future Pius X when patriarch of Venice. Their very piety, religious zeal, and charity disguised their venom.

If we welcome the fruits of liberal Catholicism a century later as nothing less than conciliar and papal teaching, were liberal Catholics right to persist in the efforts that produced such fruits, challenging papal authority at one moment, then burrowing underground, withstanding Vatican displeasure, or parrying official condemnations? Aren't we obliged to ask what those episodes teach us about the workings of the papacy, the magisterium, dissent, and the development of doctrine?

And is it sufficient to celebrate the church's embrace of liberal Catholicism's insights after 150 years of struggle, saying "all's well that ends well"? Whatever the costs of that delay to disappointed and denounced individuals, the costs to the church's integrity and mission were far graver. As I noted in my talk, in principle the late nineteenth-century and early twentieth-century church opposed aggressive nationalism, militarism, Darwinism, irrationalism, anti-Semitism, and, above all, racist neopaganism. Yet absent a robust liberal Catholicism, in nation after nation, Catholicism either aligned itself with many of these antiliberal forces or risked their triumph rather than join hands with liberals or parliamentary socialists.

Neither Cardinal George nor Father Neuhaus confronts the dark side of this history, nor did John Paul II or his successor Benedict XVI, as far as I know. It has almost become a cliché to cast the church's witness to human dignity and truth in a dramatic light by counterposing that witness to the bloody century of totalitarianisms left and right, especially as symbolized by martyred individuals or by the figure of Karol Wojtyla, struggling through Nazi and Soviet domination of Poland. Left in the shadows is the question why, when faced with the germination and birth of those terrors, whether in Germany, Italy, Spain, Portugal, Poland, Austria, or Slovakia, the church's witness proved so ineffective or ambiguous or even sometimes complicit.

In Father Neuhaus's case, the evasion of history is particularly puzzling. He claims to welcome as "wise and courageous" my analysis of liberal Catholicism, in which this history plays a major part. Yet he performs radical cosmetic surgery on that analysis, cutting away major features of the argument and adjusting other parts to resemble his own visage.

Father Neuhaus echoed, just as Cardinal George had anticipated, some of the weaknesses that I espied among liberal Catholics and their kin to the left. Cardinal George complained, for instance, that contemporary liberal Catholicism failed to develop authentic theological warrants rather than only liberal cultural grounds for proposed ecclesial changes. My worries about a slackening of intellectual rigor covered much the same ground. For Father Neuhaus, my notice of the 1960s roots of the Catholic left's style and my concern that reflexive homage to inclusiveness was eclipsing legitimate issues of Catholic identity provided springboards for his own jeremiad.

From my concerns about inattention to Catholic identity, Father Neuhaus launched a riff on the "astonishing insouciance" of "cradle Catholics of a left-liberal bent" about "the solidity and perdurance of Catholicism" and the serious harm that can be "done by unbounded criticism, conflict, and contradiction. . . . the harm of souls misled—and possibly lost—of intellectual and artistic traditions trashed, and of innumerable persons denied the high adventure of Catholic fidelity."

I would not want to back away from my point about Catholic identity for fear that it is being enlisted in a case lacking the nuance I tried to introduce. I agree with Father Neuhaus about the danger of such insouciance and about the corrosive effects on souls and traditions of "unbounded criticism, conflict, and contradiction." One of the more depressing duties in my life is a regular reading of the Letters pages in the *National Catholic Reporter*.

But it is startling to encounter the suggestion that such harsh and sweeping denunciations are a specialty of cradle Catholics of a left-liberal bent. Does Father Neuhaus watch EWTN, or peruse the columns of any number of self-declared "orthodox" publications with which he seems to be on friendly terms, or even reflect on the monthly scoldings he administers in his own journal? Does he register the tone of all too many Vatican documents? Does he worry about souls misled, constricted, repelled, alienated, or embittered by the anathemas found in those sources, or about the thinkers and scholarship caricatured, disdained, dismissed, or slandered?

It is equally startling to find this "reckless confidence" attributed to an indifference "to the incarnational reality of a Church subject to the trials, testings, distortions, inspirations, and mistakes of history." It is precisely liberal-left sensitivity to the incarnational character of a church subject to trials, testings, distortions, inspirations, and mistakes that has so often distinguished it from the reckless confidence of an ultramontane triumphalism that sees the church, the "perfect society," floating above history and human weakness.

That history did not end with Vatican II or John Paul II. What Cardinal George formulated as the task of "distinguishing the erroneous aspects of modernity from those that were compatible with, and even developments of, the Christian faith" could also be put another way: the task of distinguishing, sometimes with the help of modernity, inadequate or erroneous aspects of church teaching from what remains compatible with a developing Christian faith. Even after 1965 or after 1978, it is possible for popes, despite the guidance of the Holy Spirit, to fall into tragic error, and indeed, as I said, many liberal Catholics believe that "was probably the case in the 1968 issuance of *Humanae Vitae* and cannot be ruled out in the refusal of ordination to women."

To which Father Neuhaus briskly replies "of course this pope can and has made mistakes." When an author writes "of course," it often signals a pivotal point in the argument that he or she hopes to jam into place without further examination. Are we surprised to find that the author does not specify any of those "mistakes," nor does he indicate what a committed Catholic is to do about them? Instead, as already indicated, he launches a broad attack on liberal Catholicism and its Catholic left allies for refusing "to honestly receive the teaching of Vatican II as authoritatively interpreted by the Magisterium, and not least by the pontificate of John Paul II"—in sum, John Paul's "bold proposal of renewal."

The indictment is sweeping, but once again the crux turns out to be dissent from *Humanae Vitae*, which leads Father Neuhaus into "the question of obedience."

Although the idea of intellectual obedience may be "a scandalous one in our time," Father Neuhaus wrote, it is "an inseparable part of what it means to be Catholic."

With that I do not disagree, nor with much of the exposition that followed, about Peter, bishops, apostolic leadership, and the need to think with the church. Nor do I disagree that beyond those matters stands the relationship between freedom and truth or, further, the relationship between freely belonging and freely being bound—bound by truth, bound by love for the truth, and bound by a Catholic understanding of how the truth is made known. Finally, I do not disagree with the criticism of the modern secular liberal ideal—impossible and delusory—of the autonomous, untethered, unencumbered self.

"Given a decision between what I think the Church should teach and what the Church in fact does teach, I decide for the Church," Father Neuhaus declares. "I decide freely and rationally—because God has promised the apostolic leadership of the Church guidance and charisms that he has not promised me; because I think the Magisterium just may understand some things that I don't; because I know for sure that, in the larger picture of history, the witness of the Catholic Church is immeasurably more important than anything I might think or say. In short, I obey."

As far as it goes, this is all persuasive and, even if a little self-dramatizing, moving. Here is a man standing beneath the arches and vaults and carvings of a great cathedral, understandably awestruck, lifted up in the cloud of witnesses or maybe just hearing the still small voice. Like Job, he bows to the *tremendum.*

What is disconcerting, as so often, is less what is said than what goes unsaid. Nothing is said, for instance, about the limits to this obedience or checks against its abuse. If "intellectual obedience is a scandalous idea in our time," by no means are the reasons trivial. Pitched in such abstract and general terms—"Peter among us," Jesus' words, "He who hears you hears me," infallibility, magisterium, "the witness of the Church," freedom, truth, being bound, being "bound to be free"—there is no link in the argument that would not have served Pius IX or shackled the tongues and pens of the liberal Catholic thinkers whom Father Neuhaus, like Cardinal George, now embraces and celebrates.

What has become of the incarnational church now? The one with trials, testings, distortions, and mistakes? It is our fate to know that behind abstractions like "Peter" and "magisterium" and "witness of the church" there are real individuals, saintly or petty, ambitious or serene, thoughtful or obdurate. There are committees, factions, agendas, drafts and revisions, bargains, compromises, blacklists. . . .

It is ironic that Father Neuhaus, pointing up the consequences of liberalism's ideal of the unencumbered, autonomous self, should include the now familiar specter of "blind submission to totalitarian doctrines that present themselves as surrogates for the truth that makes us free." It seems only decent to mention that neither of the two great totalitarian doctrines of the last century had much use for liberalism or for the unencumbered, autonomous self, whatever its distance from reality. In the shadow of those doctrines, of the submission of all too many intellectuals, and of their self-denigrating confessions and recantations, there is an unsettling ring to Father Neuhaus's affirmation, "I know for sure that, in the larger picture of history, the witness of the Catholic Church is immeasurably more important than anything I might think or say. In short, I obey."

Similarly surprising and unsettling in the light of that history is Father Neuhaus's unabashed and seemingly uncritical focus on one man. All the ambiguities of Vatican II and the many questions it barely opened or left for the future have been authoritatively and definitively resolved by John Paul II. I had mentioned five areas where an effective church witness would surely demand the continuing contribution of liberal Catholicism—human sexuality, technological control over genes and the mind, relations among world religions, quantum leaps in historical consciousness and cultural pluralism, and a worldwide revolution of individual freedom and democracy. Each of them, Father Neuhaus responds, has been addressed by John Paul II, "comprehensively, repeatedly, with formidable intelligence and persuasive force." If his teaching has not been received, it is only because of recalcitrant hearers, including "liberal Catholics who incessantly pit Vatican II against the living magisterium of the Church."

Father Neuhaus wisely reminds us that the word "obedience," from *ob-audire*, contains the Latin root for "listen" or "hear." Obedience thus "means 'to give ear to, to listen to, to follow guidance.'" Is it the Catholic understanding that this process of giving ear to works only from the top down, or that one can be disobedient only from the bottom up? Can popes and bishops be disobedient by not giving ear to, not listening to lay women and men, priests, theologians, or even the secular world, by not listening to the poor, the afflicted, the vulnerable, and the excluded? And if so, what then?

Isn't obedience a matter of giving ear to, of listening to, of being guided by, many voices? The voices of God in Jesus and the Scriptures (the many voices of the Scriptures), in the sacraments and the saints, as well as the voices of pontiffs and prelates, encyclicals, catechisms, and canon law. That Catholic witness which I obey because it "is immeasurably more important than anything I might think or say" is in reality a chorus, not a single voice, and sometimes a chorus that verges on cacophony. Yes, there are rules and dispositions for listening to these voices and for authenticating them or weighing them when they appear to differ. Central to these judgments is the hierarchical authority, including the Petrine office, that God has given the church.

But that authority does not operate mechanically. When I hear it, I hear its overtones and undertones, its chords and dissonances. I hear its unanimity or its deep differences, its free exchanges or its constrained silences, its receptiveness or its defensiveness. My obedience in the faith is responsiveness, not reflex.

I believe Father Neuhaus knows this. At the conclusion of his essay, he pleads for "a conversion to *ob-audire*—to responsive listening, to lively engagement, to trustful following, to the form of reflective faith that is obedience." Liberal Catholicism would not put it differently. In principle or, I believe, in practice. Where the difference lies is, first, in liberal Catholics' conviction that, contrary to the implication of Father Neuhaus's preceding pages, this definition is compatible with serious disagreements with the papacy, including the current papacy; and, second, that Rome is no less in need of this kind of conversion than the rest of us.

Thus far, I have addressed what I think are flawed objections to liberal Catholicism in Cardinal George's original account and in Father Neuhaus's more recent critique. They both evade history. They reap where they did not sow. They welcome the incorporation of liberal Catholic stances in today's church but skirt the implications of how that came about.

Cardinal George erects a sharp wall between a liberal culture, described as incompatible with Catholicism, and liberal political and economic institutions, detachable, it seems, from that inimicable culture in the past and valuable for secular society but no longer detachable in the present or valuable for ecclesial society.

Father Neuhaus indicts liberal Catholicism, in effect, for ecclesiastical draft-dodging. His criticism rests on a fervent rendering of obedience but one that is abstract, incomplete, and inconsistent with his own professed endorsement of the liberal Catholic legacy, one in which the post-totalitarian reader searches unavailingly for the dividing line between "thinking with the church," "lively engagement," or "reflective faith," on the one hand, and irresponsible abnegation or acquiescence, on the other.

III

I do not want to conclude on these notes. Four years ago, I reflected on liberal Catholicism, not in the spirit of defense, but of critical self-examination. In that spirit, the spirit of *ob-audire*, if you will,
I would like to underscore several themes from Cardinal George and
Father Neuhaus that liberal Catholicism, along with the other challenges I previously outlined, could fruitfully hear.

One is the theme of heroism. For all the intellectual gifts of Pope
John Paul II, what resonated in his papacy, what resonates with the
young people who will never read *Veritatis Splendor* or *Fides et Ratio*,
is a call to heroism. It is a heroism rooted in Karol Wojtyla's Polish
Catholicism and its romantic literature—a heroism perhaps clearer to
our world of images and politics when a vigorous voyager-pope was
aligned with Solidarity's bold challenge to Soviet domination than
today, when a physically enfeebled man struggles with his speeches or
stamps his approval on edicts. It is a heroism nonetheless that rings
through Father Neuhaus's acclamation of the pope and consequent
paean to obedience, sacrifice, magisterium, and absorption of the individual in the larger vision.

Heroism is a tricky business. After Solidarity and the Velvet Revolution come parliamentary politics and normal existence, precisely
what all those self-consciously heroic totalitarian movements scorned.
The history of liberalism and of liberal Catholicism is filled with he-
roes and heroic moments. Yet in some ways both liberalism and liberal
Catholicism are antiheroic. They are sensible, balanced, practical, everyday, Appolonian rather than Dionysian. The heroic is more often
celebrated on the Catholic left, among the allies I criticized rather
extensively, than among liberal Catholics.

Liberal Catholicism must have a more comprehending attitude
toward the heroic. That is my first theme.

The second is joy. Nothing in Cardinal George's original remarks,
to which my wife responded, made me gasp as much as his declaration
that liberal Catholicism had proven inadequate in "fostering the joyful
self-surrender called for in Christian marriage, in consecrated life, in
ordained priesthood." On what empirical basis did the archbishop

generalize about joyful self-surrender in liberal Catholic marriages? Were there statistics measuring liberal Catholic self-surrender rates, or even divorce rates? I myself had known of some conservative Catholic marriages where whatever self-surrendering went on gave every sign of being pretty unjoyful, if not destructively bitter. In truth my puny sample regarding such a private, mysterious matter, just like my address book of joyfully self-sacrificing liberal Catholic priests and religious, provided no grounds whatsoever for generalizing, and I couldn't imagine doing so. Wasn't this a classic case of Catholic a priori reasoning? Liberal Catholics had notoriously rejected the condemnation of contraceptive sex in marriage. Only noncontraceptive sex in marriage could be joyful self-surrender. Ergo. . . .

I cannot say that my reaction to his assertions has changed. But liberal Catholicism should nonetheless take to its heart his underscoring of joy and joyfulness. Liberal Catholicism has not been notable, certainly in embattled recent years, for joyfulness. I am not sure who has. But it has every reason to see itself in one of the phrases Cardinal George used to describe "simply Catholicism": "a faith joyful in all the gifts Christ wants to give us and open to the whole world he died to save."

Finally, I want to retain the theme of obedience—giving ear to, responsive listening, lively engagement, trustful following, reflective faith, all the phrases Father Neuhaus happily contributed. An embattled state is as little conducive to these as to joy.

Yet embattled we are. The framework for a healthy heroism, a sustaining joyfulness, and a receptive listening will not be found in a restored emphasis on following orders, personal abnegation, or intellectual disavowal. It will be found, I suggest, in a zone of daily prayer, sacramental habits, household rituals, continuing study, and physical reminders and expressions of our faith—something like the apparently dreaded Catholic subculture of recent memory but stressing affirmations of what we are rather than negations of what others are. Within such a zone, the heroism of everyday life can be made manifest, the springs of joy can be refreshed, and the voices of authority can be heard and engaged in security. There would be sufficient shelter for the play of irony, the exertion of intellectual struggle, and the negotiation of identity I have previously urged on liberal Catholicism.

These are only a few light strokes sketching the goal of a different kind of Catholic subculture, positive not punitive, structured but permeable, defined but not defensive. A little liberal, if you will, but also a little conservative. Perhaps it cannot be created. If it can be, only liberal Catholicism will do it.

CHAPTER 10

The Faith of a Theologian

AVERY CARDINAL DULLES, S.J.

I n the letter inviting me to accept the Marianist Award for the year 2004, your president, Dr. Curran, suggested that I might take the occasion to speak of the relationship of faith to my own scholarly work. The proposal immediately captured my fancy since faith and theology have been, so to speak, the two poles of my existence. The subject, besides, has considerable importance for our time and place, because many of the difficulties we experience in Church and society are due to the impoverishment of faith or to theology that is not in harmony with faith.

From their first beginnings my religious convictions have been intimately bound up with my intellectual life. In my prep school days, whatever faith I had was eroded by instructors, assigned readings, and personal study. The evidence available to me seemed to indicate that if God existed at all, there was no real function for such a being. Everything seemed to be explicable in principle by natural causes and human agency. The study of human and cosmic origins, I believed, had done away with any need for the hypothesis of a Divine Creator or of a Provident Governor of the Universe. The materialistic evolutionism that captivated me in those years is still widespread in our day and seriously harmful to faith.

In my first years in college the question that continually haunted me was whether my life had any real meaning. Were human beings with their rationality misfits in the universe? Was reason a source of alienation in a universe that existed without meaning or purpose? I was almost prepared to admit that it was foolish to ask the question why anything existed, since objective reasons were a figment of the mind. But my study of Greek philosophy rescued me from this dismal conclusion. Plato gave good grounds for holding that mind, not matter, was at the origin of all things. Aristotle made it clear that the laws of reason were in conformity with those of being. What was absurd in logic was impossible in reality. From this it followed that there was a correlation between being and intelligibility. The more being a thing had, the more intelligible it was. Matter, as the lowest grade of being, was only minimally intelligible. In this way I was able to turn materialism on its head.

I was particularly concerned with the moral order. Was it reasonable to respect the rights of others when it did not suit one's own convenience? Could I be morally obliged to sacrifice my own advantage and even my own life for the sake of some higher good? Plato convinced me that such sacrifices could be commendable and indeed mandatory. It was always better, he said, to suffer evil than to do evil. As soon as I accepted that principle I became convinced that the moral order had a transcendent source. An absolute obligation could come only from an absolute being. And it seemed reasonable to hold, as Plato surmised, that virtue would be rewarded and vice punished in a future life. The logic of Plato's position pointed to something very like the Christian God. Right reason therefore opened up for me the path to faith.

Although I took several philosophy courses in college, I was not a philosophy major. My field of concentration was the cultural history of medieval and Renaissance Europe. This branch of study made me conscious that all the cultural and political institutions of the West were deeply indebted to the great Christian civilization of the first millennium. That civilization was built on two pillars: the natural wisdom of Greece and Rome and the revealed religion of the Bible. The combination of the two was immeasurably richer than either taken in isolation. Biblical revelation in many ways completed and confirmed the philosophical probings of Greece and Rome. Conversely, the early Christians, seeking to understand what they held by faith, received inestimable help from the wisdom of pre-Christian antiquity.

During my four years in college I did not take a single course in religion or theology, but I learned a good deal about both through history, literature, and the arts. I found deep spiritual nourishment in reading Augustine, Bernard, Thomas Aquinas, and Dante. In my senior year I wrote a thesis that was published the following year as my first book: a study of the Italian lay theologian Giovanni Pico della Mirandola, in relation to the Scholastic tradition.[1] As I did my research for this thesis I found myself bitten by the theological bug. My supreme interest would never again be anything but theology.

Attracted though I was toward the Middle Ages and the Renaissance, I had to admit that the past could not be resurrected. But I was thrilled to discover that it had never really died. Much of what I admired in pre-Reformation Europe was still present and vibrant in the Catholic Church. As a college undergraduate I discovered the writings of Etienne Gilson and Jacques Maritain, two living French Thomist philosophers. I read as many books by each of them as I could find, sometimes in the French original before the translations were available. Shunning antiquarianism, these two thinkers were well versed not only in medieval but also in modern and contemporary thought. They pointed out how modern philosophy had lost its way and fallen victim to individualism and skepticism. I came to look upon Immanuel Kant as the crucial figure who marked the death of metaphysics and the birth of the positivism, historicism, pragmatism, and subjectivism of later centuries.

Harvard College, where I was studying, was in no way a Catholic institution, but the professors under whom I studied did not disguise their admiration for figures such as Gilson and Maritain. Gilson had taught at Harvard several years earlier and had delivered one of the principal lectures at the university's tercentenary celebration in 1935.

Gilson and Maritain were only two of a great cloud of witnesses. To my delight I discovered a Catholic bookstore and lending library where I was able to find an ample supply of literature, especially by writers of the Catholic Renaissance that had been thriving in England since the days of G. K. Chesterton and Hilaire Belloc. Each weekend I would borrow an armful of books by authors such as C. C. Martindale, E. I. Watkin, Ronald Knox, Martin D'Arcy, and Arnold Lunn.

They convinced me that the wisdom of Catholicism could make a much-needed contribution to the world in our day.

In addition to my historical studies at Harvard and my personal reading in contemporary Catholic thought, a third stream fed into my conversion: the actual life of the Church in Cambridge, Massachusetts. The Catholic parishes were bustling with activity. Sunday Masses were crowded, and weekday Masses early each morning were well attended by ordinary people on their way to work. Special occasions such as Holy Week were celebrated with great solemnity—conducted, of course, in Latin. I vividly remember one Sunday evening when I stumbled by accident upon a service that turned out to be the Benediction of the Blessed Sacrament. A large congregation of working-class people was singing Latin hymns such as the "O Salutaris" and the "Pange Lingua," which I recognized as the work of Thomas Aquinas. Here, most evidently, was the Church to which I must belong!

I have spoken at greater length than I intended of the process by which I came to the Church, but those years were formative in a way that no others could be for me. For most of us, I suspect, our attitudes and convictions are basically formed by our experiences before the age of twenty-two. However that may be, I must say that my own perspectives on faith and reason were shaped during my undergraduate days. I do not see how I could give a proper account of my theological orientations without reference to this background.

Bypassing my time in law school and the Navy, I pass now to my years as a Jesuit, which fall into two segments: before and after my completion of graduate studies. I studied philosophy from 1948 to 1951 and taught that subject at Fordham University from 1951 to 1953. The philosophy that I learned and tried to teach was a form of neo-Thomism not unlike that of Gilson and Maritain. As a philosophical system it was closely correlated with Catholic faith. This harmony strikes me as a strong asset, since as a believer I could not appropriate any philosophy that did not mesh with my religious convictions. I could not have accepted idealism, materialism, atheism, agnosticism, or pragmatism as a philosophical base for my thought, although I might be able to learn something from these systems.

Scholasticism in its various forms had been built up by generations of Christian believers, among whom Thomas Aquinas holds a preeminent place. His philosophy, of course, is not beyond criticism. No philosophical system can be made a matter of faith. But no other philosophy has rivaled his in its fruitfulness for theology.

As a theologian I make use of elements from several philosophical systems. St. Thomas, in my opinion, did the same. He could write at times like a Neoplatonist and at other times like a strict Aristotelian. He could also borrow ideas from Stoics and from Jewish and Arabic philosophers when they served his purposes. I have found it possible to adhere essentially to the metaphysics of St. Thomas, modifying it to some extent to make room for the personalism of modern Thomists such as Jean Mouroux, W. Norris Clarke, and Pope John Paul II. For epistemological questions I draw freely from the work of John Henry Newman and Michael Polanyi, while amending them to make room for a stronger metaphysical realism than theirs.

I began my formal studies in theology at Woodstock, Maryland, in 1953. Our courses in dogmatic theology were based predominantly on the work of twentieth-century Jesuits of the Roman school, who followed Suárez, de Lugo, Bellarmine, and other Jesuits of the baroque period. Heavily influenced by Thomas Aquinas, these theologians did not hesitate to go beyond the letter of his teaching in grappling with questions that he had left open. This style of theology has gone somewhat out of fashion since Vatican II, but I am grateful to have been immersed in it. It gave me a thorough exposure to the classical theological questions and debates.

For me and my fellow students at Woodstock the classroom instruction was not the centerpiece of our theological education. The mid-1950s, when we were privileged to study, were perhaps the most exciting years of the century for Catholic theology. In France, de Lubac, Daniélou, and Congar, among others, were developing the theology of ressourcement, sometimes labeled *la nouvelle théologie*. In Germany Karl Adam and Romano Guardini were at the height of their careers. Karl Rahner, Hans Urs von Balthasar, and Bernard Lonergan were achieving prominence. Like many of my fellow students, I eagerly devoured the writings of these thinkers. And at Woodstock, I should add, we could not avoid some involvement in the issues of church and state, since John Courtney Murray was in residence as editor of *Theological Studies*.

Other aspects of the theological renewal after the Second World War should be mentioned in this connection. The biblical movement was thriving, with the Pontifical Biblical Commission relaxing the old antimodernist prohibitions and opening the way for source criticism, form criticism, and redaction criticism. The catechetical movement was vibrant, inspired by the kerygmatic theology of Jungmann and Hofinger. The theology of the laity was getting off to a strong start, led by Yves Congar and Gustave Thils. I personally developed a strong interest in the ecumenical movement, which was beginning to capture the interest of Catholics in Western Europe and even in the United States. A year after being ordained I briefly visited Paris, Louvain, and Innsbruck, and then spent the year in Germany, where I was able to make contact with many of the leading ecumenists, both Protestant and Catholic. Then I went to Rome in 1958 for my doctoral studies, and wrote a dissertation on the ecclesial status of Protestant churches according to Catholic theology—a theme that prepared me well for the Second Vatican Council.

If time permitted, I could say a great deal about my work as a theologian and teacher in the last forty years of the twentieth century. To be as brief as possible, I would say that my work was centered on Vatican II. By 1960, when I started teaching theology, preparations for the Council were in full swing. From Woodstock we followed every step in the conciliar debates with passionate interest. In the first decade after the Council I was heavily engaged in ecumenical dialogues and in interpreting the Council documents to Catholic audiences.

In all my theological endeavors I have striven to keep the relationship between theology and faith intact. For me theology depends on faith, for it is nothing other than a systematic effort to understand the nature, contents, and implications of faith. By faith I mean a free and trusting assent to the Word of God (*logos theou*). Faith is divine to the extent that it responds to that Word. Theology of any kind presupposes divine faith as the condition for its existence. Christian theology rests on specifically Christian faith, inasmuch as it recognizes Christ as the incarnate Word of God. Catholic theology presupposes Catholic faith, because it accepts the authoritative mediation of the Church with her scriptures and traditions. Christian and Catholic theology, therefore, rest upon Christian and Catholic faith. If the faith is denied at any of these three levels, theology ceases to be Catholic, to be Christian, and even to be theology at all.

I am aware that some authors have maintained that theology can be done without faith. Nonbelievers, I suppose, could discuss what they might hold if they believed that there were a God or that he had spoken through Christ and the Church. But this would only be a kind of hypothetical discourse, based on a contrary-to-fact condition. No one but the believer is in a position to affirm theological propositions as true. The same propositions might be affirmed by the nonbeliever on other grounds, but in their case the affirmation would not be theological. Faith is what distinguishes theology from other disciplines such as philosophy, history, psychology, and sociology, which deal with some of the same materials.

All theologians, then, must be believers, but not all believers are theologians. Intelligent believers always and inevitably reflect on their faith and in so doing engage in an informal kind of theology, but only a trained theologian can give carefully reasoned statements about matters of faith. In modern times the term "theology" has come to mean an academic discipline conducted within a community of faith. The theologian is expected to be familiar with the Bible and with the history of doctrines, to be capable of articulating the contents of faith in a systematic way, and to be professionally equipped to answer questions about faith.

Whatever my merits and limitations may be, I am a theologian in the strict sense just described. My religious superiors commissioned me to engage in theological study on the doctoral level and assigned me to teach theological subjects. I am grateful to them for having done so, because in my undergraduate days, as already mentioned, I was bit by the theological bug. Since the age of twenty I have looked upon God as the ultimate source and goal of my life, and have considered my relationship to him far more interesting and important than any other relationship. What could be more intriguing and absorbing than to ponder God's message of salvation?

I can well understand that other academics might be more attracted to art, music, literature, science, history, philosophy, or some other discipline. I have felt these attractions myself, but even as a theologian I can engage in them to some extent. Theology makes use of many other disciplines as aids in interpreting the Word of God and in inducing people to accept and obey that Word.

Theology, as I understand it, is not only an exercise of faith; it is conducted in the service of faith—that of the individual and of the Church as the community of faith. As the Congregation for the Doctrine of the Faith explains in its admirable instruction on "The Ecclesial Vocation of the Theologian" (1990), the theologian's work corresponds to a dynamism found in the faith itself. Truth, once lodged in the human mind, seeks to be understood and communicated.

As a priest I have felt a responsibility to serve the pastoral mission of the Church, adapting my work to the needs and problems of the day. In the years immediately following Vatican II, the overriding need seemed to be to explain to the Catholic faithful how there could be such things as change and reform in the Church. My principal adversary then was a static traditionalist mentality that would not relinquish the rigid and polemical attitudes that had become ingrained since the Counter-Reformation. I sensed that the Church as a living community must adapt her manner of thinking, speaking, and acting to the current situation, while of course preserving all that belongs to revelation itself.

The apologists for Vatican II, with whom I associated myself, won over the minds of most American Catholics. But since about 1975 an equal and opposite problem has arisen. Under the pressure of the historical and cultural relativism that dominates the secular culture of our day, some Christians and Catholics have lost confidence in the permanent and universal value of revealed truth. It has become necessary to insist against this trend that Jesus Christ is the same yesterday, today, and forever, and that the contents of Christian and Catholic faith, definitively taught by the Church, are infallibly and irreformably true.

The current trend toward historical and cultural relativism is a much more serious threat than the immobilism of the traditionalists. The traditionalists, while they were in error theologically, had unquestioning faith in the word of God and in the creeds and dogmas of the Church. Relativism, however, treats every proposition as if it were valid at most for its own time and place. For this reason it directly challenges Christian and Catholic faith, which adheres to the dogmas of the Church as abidingly valid truths. Relativism is also an obstacle to evangelization, which several recent popes have ranked as a high priority. For the relativists, Christian believers may call on Jesus as their Lord and God, but they dare not claim that he is Lord of all. The Congregation for the Doctrine of the Faith clearly pointed to the pitfalls of relativism in its declaration *Dominus Iesus*, issued in 2000.

The problem of dissent became acute after the publication of *Humanae Vitae* in 1968. I never dissented from that encyclical nor, if my memory serves me, from any other Catholic doctrine. But I tried to explain to orthodox believers how it was possible for a Catholic, without rejecting the faith, to dissent from certain noninfallible teachings. Such dissent, I maintained, must for any good Catholic be rare, reluctant, and respectful. I never associated myself with collective protests in which the teaching of the Church was publicly denied. Such actions, I believe, inevitably harm the Church by discrediting the magisterium.

In what precedes I have tried to show how theology in general, and my theology in particular, depends on faith and is in service to faith. Faith is the sine qua non of theology. But questions can still be raised about whether theology supports and strengthens faith, or, on the contrary, challenges and weakens it. Even at its best, theology encounters difficulties in its effort to master the truth of revelation, because the mysteries of faith so exceed the capacities of any created intellect that they tend to baffle and disorient the mind. Every theologian, I suspect, experiences moments of perplexity in trying to construct a rationale for Christian faith and give a coherent interpretation to doctrines such as the Trinity, the Incarnation, and the Real Presence of Christ in the Eucharist. But in the end it is possible to attain a synthesis between faith and reason in which the mind can rest peacefully.

The First Vatican Council teaches that reason illuminated by faith can achieve by God's grace a very fruitful, though limited, understanding of revelation. This understanding, it declared, rests on the connection of the revealed mysteries with one another, on the analogy between them and the objects of natural knowledge, and on the connection of the mysteries with the last end to which the human spirit is oriented.[2] Pope John Paul II, in his encyclical on Faith and Reason, points out how faith reinforces reason and enables it to discover horizons that it could not reach on its own.[3] This expectation is not unrealistic. Our Catholic tradition affords splendid examples of such theological achievements.

Theology, however, can go astray. Most of the great heresies have grown out of theological errors. Even when orthodox, theology can be less than helpful. Over the centuries, theologians have stirred up controversy and dissension in the Church. They have frequently fallen victim to a *rabies theologica*, a kind of theological fury, in attacking one another. The most orthodox theologians have sometimes engaged in savage polemics. In their zeal for truth they tend to disregard the Christian virtues of tact, civility, and charity.

Even with the best of intentions, theology can put difficulties in the way of faith. I experienced this in one of my courses as a student. In apologetics we were taught that our faith rested upon the Gospels, which could not be defended unless they could be shown to be strictly historical documents and to contain eyewitness reports of the words and deeds of Jesus. The proofs offered for these theses seemed very unconvincing, at least to me. Fortunately, however, I learned in Scripture courses that the Gospels, composed a generation or two after the death of Jesus, were theological documents attesting to the faith of the early Church. Reliably communicating what it was important for the faithful to know about Jesus, the Gospels were not to be read as if they were verbatim reports. In this way my Scripture courses spared me from undergoing a crisis of faith.

In a wholly different way, certain more recent trends in contemporary Catholic theology may be corrosive of faith. Ecumenical and interreligious dialogues have sometimes led theologians into the trap of dogmatic compromises. Liberation theology, while it could be authentically Christian and Catholic, sometimes took over too much of the social analysis of Marxism.

I should like to call special attention to the problems inherent in the so-called "theology from below" that is sometimes practiced in Christology and ecclesiology. While the term means different things to different authors, such theology often confines its vision to purely human and historical phenomena. In Christology it concentrates so intensely on the humanity of Jesus that it puts his divinity in brackets. The method tends to dismiss on principle those passages in the Gospels that would be incredible if Jesus were a mere man—some of his miracles, for example, and his divine claims. Walter Kasper puts his finger on the difficulty when he writes:

> A Christology purely "from below" is therefore condemned to failure. Jesus understands himself "from above" in his whole human existence. The transition from anthropological to theological viewpoint cannot therefore be carried out without a break. A decisive change of standpoint is required.[4]

Just as a Christology from below, taken alone, falls short of Christian faith, so does an ecclesiology from below, left to itself. Faith teaches that Holy Scripture is divinely inspired, that Catholic tradition has divine authority, that the Church is the Body of Christ, and that Christ abides with his Church and with the successors of the apostles, assisting them in their mission till the end of time. These assurances enable us to find the word of God in Scripture and tradition and to trust the magisterium, confident that God will not allow his Church to betray the truth committed to it. An ecclesiology from below typically treats Scripture as a merely human document, looks upon tradition as mere folklore, and calls into question the solemn teaching of popes and councils. Joseph Ratzinger, now Pope Benedict XVI, points out a real danger when he writes:

The ecclesiology from "below" which is commended to us today presupposes that one regards the Church as a purely sociological quantity and that Christ as an acting subject has no real significance. But in this case, one is no longer speaking about a church at all but about a society which has also set its religious goals in itself. According to the logic of this position, such a church will also be "below" in a theological sense, namely "of this world," which is how Jesus defines below in the Gospel of John (Jn 8:23).[5]

Because I cannot accept any split between faith and theology, I have always practiced theology on the assumption that Christ is the divine Son and that he makes himself accessible though the privileged testimony of Scripture, tradition, and the living Church. To work on other principles is to violate the nature of theology as a reflection on faith from within faith. Theological speculation that adopts naturalistic premises eats away at the faith of God's people.

Critical reasoning, to be sure, has a legitimate place in theology. But criticism itself must always be based on principles and presuppositions. In a theology from below, the critic methodologically excludes the supernatural and adopts a pre-Christian posture. This approach may be an admissible form of religious inquiry but has not yet risen to the status of theology. Catholic theology begins in the fullness of Catholic faith.

As I believe I have shown in the early part of this lecture, pre-theological disciplines can serve as pedagogues on the journey to faith. My studies in philosophy and history brought me to the very verge of faith. Conscious of this, I have retained a lifelong interest in apologetics, which aims to show the plausibility of faith to those who do not yet believe. But the apologist, to accomplish this task effectively, must be a person of faith.

Faith, then, is the presupposition and the animating principle of anything that claims to be theology. And faith is a gift. One may prepare for it, dispose oneself for it, and pray for it, but only God can confer it. For those who understand what faith is, there are only two reasonable attitudes. If they have faith, they should treasure it and pray for the added gift of perseverance. And if they lack it, they should long for the gift and pray to receive it.

Since I began to write theology I have considered nothing more important than orthodoxy. However brilliant it may be, theology that deviates from faith is, in my judgment, worse than useless. Theology is not the master but the servant of faith. Theologians should be grateful to be corrected by higher authority. They should not imagine that it is their mission to sit in judgment on the magisterium.

I cannot claim that I have completely lived up to the principles set forth in this lecture. That will be for others to judge. Not only my earlier writings but even the most recent may be in need of correction. St. Augustine in his senior years set a good example for the rest of us by writing his *Retractationes*. I might be inclined to follow him if only I had the assurance that I have advanced in wisdom and grace as I have advanced in years.

Notes

INTRODUCTION

CATHOLIC INTELLECTUALS: NO IVORY TOWER

JAMES L. HEFT, S.M.

1. James L. Heft, S.M., ed., *Faith and the Intellectual Life* (Notre Dame, IN: University of Notre Dame Press, 1996).

2. For example, Alan Sica, a leading social theorist at Pennsylvania State University, included Charles Taylor's lecture, "A Catholic Modernity?" under the title of "Charles Taylor's Marianist Award Lecture" in a section of social theorists entitled "Postmodernism, Globalization, and the New Century," in *Social Thought: From the Enlightenment to the Present* (Boston: Pearson, 2004). Taylor's lecture, the first in this new series, became itself the cornerstone of an edited volume, *A Catholic Modernity?* (New York: Oxford University Press, 1996).

3. Denys Turner, *Faith Seeking* (London: SCM Press, 2002), 136.

4. Mark Roche, *The Intellectual Appeal of Catholicism and the Idea of a Catholic University* (Notre Dame, IN: University of Notre Dame Press, 2003), 6–7.

1. A CATHOLIC MODERNITY?
CHARLES TAYLOR

1. This is not to say that we cannot claim in certain areas to have gained certain insights and settled certain questions which still troubled our ancestors. For instance, we are able to see the Inquisition clearly for the unevangelical horror that it was. But this doesn't exclude our having

a lot to learn from earlier ages as well, even from people who also made the mistake of supporting the Inquisition.

2. Henri Bremond, *Histoire littéraire du sentient religieux en France depuis la fin des guerres de religion jusqu'à nos jours* (Paris: A. Colin, 1967–68).

3. See Charles Taylor, *Sources of the Self* (Cambridge, MA: Harvard University Press, 1989), chap. 13.

4. See, e.g., Daniel Callahan, *Setting Limits: Medical Goals in an Aging Society* (Washington, DC: Georgetown University Press, 1995).

5. James Miller, *The Passion of Michel Foucault* (New York: Simon and Schuster, 1993).

6. See René Girard, *La Violence et le Sacré* (Paris: Grasset, 1972); and *Le Bouc Emissaire* (Paris: Grasset, 1982).

7. Fyodor Dostoyevsky, *The Devils,* trans. David Magarshack (Harmondsworth, Middlesex: Penguin, 1971), 404.

8. Which I have discussed in Charles Taylor, *The Malaise of Modernity* (Toronto: Anansi, 1991); American edition: *The Ethics of Authenticity* (Cambridge, MA: Harvard University Press, 1992).

9. See *Ethics of Authenticity.*

4. MEMOIRS AND MEANING
JILL KER CONWAY

1. Jane Addams, *Twenty Years at Hull-House* (Champaign: University of Illinois Press, 1910), *The Second Twenty Years at Hull-House* (New York: Macmillan, 1930); M. Carey Thomas's diaries and letters are quoted extensively in Helen Lefkowitz Horowitz, *The Power and Passion of M. Carey Thomas* (Champaign: University of Illinois Press, 1994); Florence Kelley, *Notes of Sixty Years: The Autobiograph of Florence Kelly* (Chicago: Charles H. Kerr, 1986); Alice Hamilton, *Exploring the Dangerous Trades* (Boston: Little, Brown, 1943).

2. Addams, *Twenty Years at Hull-House*, 85.

3. See James D. Watson, *The Double Helix* (New York: Touchstone, 1968); Lee Iacocca with William Novak, *Iacocca: An Autobiography* (New York: Bantam Reissue, 1986); Henry Ford, *My Life and Work* (Garden City, NY: Doubleday, 1922).

4. Georges Gusdorf, "Conditions and Limits of Autobiography," trans. in James Olney, *Autobiography, Essays Theoretical and Critical* (Princeton: Princeton University Press, 1980).

5. Job 13: 13–15, 17–20, 22, *New Oxford Annotated Bible* (New York: Oxford University Press, 2001).

6. Jill Ker Conway, *When Memory Speaks: Reflections on Autobiography* (New York: Knopf, 1998), 176–77.

5. CATHOLIC AND INTELLECTUAL: CONJUNCTION OR DISJUNCTION?
MARCIA L. COLISH

1. John Henry Newman, *The Idea of a University* (New York: Oxford University Press, 1976), 110–12.

2. Ibid., 213.

3. Ibid., 197.

4. Ibid., 198.

5. Jaroslav Pelikan, *The Idea of a University: A Reexamination* (New Haven: Yale University Press, 1992), 54–55.

6. Augustine, *On Christian Doctrine*, 2.40.60, trans. D. W. Robertson (Indianapolis: Bobbs-Merrill, 1958), 75–76, paraphrasing Exodus 3:22.

7. Cassiodorus, *Institutes*, 1.27.2, trans. Leslie Webber Jones (New York: Octagon Books, 1966), 127.

8. Hugh of St. Victor, *Didascalicon*, 6.3, trans. Jerome Taylor (New York: Columbia University Press, 1961), 137.

9. On this principle, see Henri de Lubac, "A propos de la formule: *diversi sed non adversi,*" *Mélanges Jules Lebreton-Recherches de science religieuse* 40 (1952): 27–40; Hubert Silvestre, "'Diversi sed non adversi,'" *Recherches de théologie ancienne et médiévale* 31 (1964): 24–32.

6. CATHOLICISM AND HUMAN RIGHTS
MARY ANN GLENDON

1. Mary Ann Glendon, *A World Made New: Eleanor Roosevelt and the Universal Declaration of Human Rights* (New York: Random House, 2001). Unless otherwise specified, the references herein to the history of the Universal Declaration are drawn from *A World Made New*.

2. Dorothy Day, *The Long Loneliness* (New York: Harper and Brothers, 1952).

3. Avery Dulles, "Human Rights: The United Nations and Papal Teaching" (Laurence J. McGinley Lecture, Fordham University, November 18, 1998), 4.

4. H. G. Wells, *The Rights of Man, or What Are We Fighting For?* (Middlesex: Penguin, 1940).

5. UDHR, Preamble and Articles 1, 16, 22, 25, and 26.

6. *Populorum Progressio*, 13.

7. John P. Humphrey, *Human Rights and the United Nations: A Great Adventure* (Dobbs Ferry, NY: Transnational Publishing, 1984), 65–66.

8. *On the Edge of Greatness: The Diaries of John Humphrey*, vol. 1, A. J. Hobbins, ed. (Montreal: McGill University Libraries, 1994), 87.

9. René Cassin, "Vatican II et la Protection de la Personne," 13 *Journal des Communautés* 17 (1966).

10. *Pacem in Terris*, 143.

11. E.g., Michel Villey, *Le Droit et les Droits de l'Homme* (Paris: Presses Universitaires de France, 1983).

12. John Finnis, *Natural Law and Natural Rights* (New York: Oxford University Press, 1980).

13. *Centesimus Annus*, 46.

14. See Giorgio Filibeck, "Human Rights in the Teachings of John Paul II: Bases and Principles," 46 *Al Abhath: Journal of the Faculty of Arts and Sciences, American University of Beirut* (1998); *Human Rights in the Teaching of the Church: From John XXIII to John Paul II* (Vatican City: Libreria Editrice Vaticana, 1994).

15. Address to the United Nations, Oct. 2, 1979, 7; Address to the United Nations, Oct. 5, 1995, 2.

16. Dulles, "Human Rights," 12.

17. *Gaudium et Spes*, 41.

18. John Paul II, World Day of Peace Message 1998, 2.

19. Hannah Arendt, *The Origins of Totalitarianism* (New York: Meridian, 1958), 374.

7. A FEELING FOR HIERARCHY
MARY DOUGLAS

1. I thank Richard Fardon whose biography *Mary Douglas* (New York: Routledge, 1999) drew together these scattered threads and convinced me that there was a central theme.

2. Benjamin Schwartz, *The World of Thought in Ancient China* (Cambridge, MA: Belknap Press, 1989).

3. Indeed in that period of the 1920s, a friend, the daughter of missionaries in China, who was also sent home told me that there was a heavy toll of child mortality if they stayed with the parents.

4. Teresa Watkin, Heather Bowman, Joan Remers, and myself.

5. Mary Douglas, *The Lele of the Kasai* (London: International African Institute, 1963).

6. Douglas, *Purity and Danger: An Analysis of Concepts of Pollution and Taboo* (London: Routledge, 1966).

7. Douglas, *Natural Symbols* (New York: Pantheon Books, 1970).

8. Mary Douglas and Baron Isherwood, *The World of Goods* (New York, Basic Books, 1979).

9. Michael Thompson, Richard Ellis, and Aaron Wildavsky, *Cultural Theory* (Boulder, CO: Westview Press, 1990).

10. I mention this to acknowledge the profound questions from the University of Dayton audience, and in particular this one about the tension between hierarchy and individualism from Sean Wilkinson. I hope I have incorporated answers to them in this revised version of the talk.

11. Douglas, ed., *Food in the Social Order* (New York: Russell Sage Foundation, 1984).

12. Mary Douglas and Aaron Wildavsky, *Risk and Culture* (Berkeley: University of California Press, 1982); Douglas, *Risk Acceptability according to the Social Sciences* (New York: Russell Sage Foundation, 1986); Douglas, *Risk and Blame* (New York: Routledge, 1992).

13. Douglas, *How Institutions Think* (Syracuse: Syracuse University Press, 1986); *Thought Styles* (London: Sage, 1996); Mary Douglas and Steven Ney, *Missing Persons* (Berkeley: University of California Press, 1998).

14. *In the Wilderness: The Doctrine of Defilement in the Book of Numbers* (Sheffield: Sheffield Academic Press, 1993; paperback, Oxford University Press, 2001).

15. *Leviticus as Literature* (Oxford and New York: Oxford University Press, 1999).

16. I should put on record my deep gratitude to the Bible scholars who were so generous with their time and patience, putting up with my ignorance and encouraging me to persevere with these studies which they made more exciting for me than anything I had ever done before.

8. MY LIFE AS A "WOMAN": EDITING THE WORLD
MARGARET O'BRIEN STEINFELS

1. Anthony Giddens, *Modernity and Self-Identity* (Cambridge: Polity Press, 1991), 20.

2. See Sandra Schneiders, *With Oil in Their Lamps: Faith, Feminism, and the Future* (New York: Paulist Press, 2000), 29.

9. LIBERAL CATHOLICISM REEXAMINED
PETER STEINFELS

1. Pope Pius IX, *Syllabus of Errors* (Dec. 8, 1864), para. 80.

2. The analysis of liberal Catholicism here is developed further in my essay, "The Failed Encounter: the Catholic Church and Liberalism in the Nineteenth Century," in R. Bruce Douglass and David Hollenbach, editors, *Catholicism and Liberalism* (New York: Cambridge University Press, 1994), 19–44, and rest on the references given there.

3. Founded in 1926 by Australian lawyer Francis Joseph Sheed and his British wife Maisie Ward, Sheed and Ward is one of the most eminent Catholic publishing houses in the world today. In its now seventy-seven-year history, Sheed and Ward have published some of the most prominent names in Catholic thought. It is currently under the ownership of Rowman and Littlefield Publishers, Inc.

4. Peter Steinfels, "Reinventing Liberal Catholicism," *Commonweal*, Nov. 19, 1999, 30–39.

5. David J. O'Brien, "What Happened to the Catholic Left?" in Mary Jo Weaver, editor, *What's Left?* (Bloomington: Indiana University Press, 1999), 25–82.

6. As a Lutheran clergyman, Father Neuhaus was for seventeen years senior pastor of a low-income African-American parish in Brooklyn, New York. Father Neuhaus has played a leadership role in organizations dealing with civil rights, international justice, and ecumenism. In September 1991, he was ordained a priest of the Archdiocese of New York. Father Neuhaus serves as president of the Institute on Religion and Public Life, a nonpartisan interreligious research and education institute in New York City. He is also editor-in-chief of the Institute's publication, *First Things: A Monthly Journal of Religion and Public Life.*

7. Cardinal George's critique can be found in the same anniversary issue of *Commonweal*: Francis George, "How Liberalism Fails the Church," *Commonweal*, Nov. 19, 1999, 24–29. The issue also contains responses to both Cardinal George's and my articles, by John Noonan, John T. McGreevy, and E. J. Dionne. Father Neuhaus's critique is found in Richard John Neuhaus, "The Persistence of the Catholic Moment," *First Things*, February 2003, 26–30.

10. THE FAITH OF A THEOLOGIAN
AVERY CARDINAL DULLES, S.J.

1. Avery Dulles, *Princeps Concordiae: Pico della Mirandola and the Scholastic Tradition* (Cambridge, MA: Harvard University Press, 1941).

2. Denzinger-Schoenmetzer, par. 3016.

3. *Fides et Ratio*, par. 67.

4. Walter Kasper, *Jesus the Christ* (New York: Paulist, 1976), 247.

5. Joseph Ratzinger, "Communio: A Program," *Communio* 19 (1992): 436–49, at 445.

Contributors

JAMES L. HEFT, S.M.

James L. Heft, S.M., is University Professor of Faith and Culture and Chancellor at the University of Dayton. In 1977 he received his doctorate from the University of Toronto in Historical Theology. He served as Chair of the Religious Studies Department at the University of Dayton from 1983 to 1989 and as Provost from 1989 to 1996, at which time he was appointed to his current position. He also devotes much of his time to the Institute for Advanced Catholic Studies at the University of Southern California, of which his is the President and Founding Director. He is the author of *John XXII (1316–1334) and Papal Teaching Authority* (1986) and has edited *Faith and the Intellectual Life* (1996), *A Catholic Modernity? An Essay by Charles Taylor* (1999), and *Beyond Violence: Religious Sources for Social Transformation* (Fordham University Press, 2004).

Currently, Father Heft is working on a book on Catholic higher education. His article "Mary of Nazareth, Feminism and the Tradition," co-authored with Una Cadegan, won the 1990 Catholic Press Association award for best scholarly article. He has authored over 150 articles and book chapters and serves on the editorial board of two journals. He has served on numerous boards and most recently chaired the board of directors of the Association of Catholic Colleges and Universities.

AVERY CARDINAL DULLES, S.J.

Avery Cardinal Dulles, S.J., an internationally known author and lecturer, is the Laurence J. McGinley Professor of Religion and Society at Fordham University, a position he has held since 1988. Cardinal Dulles received the doctorate in sacred theology from the Gregorian University in Rome in 1960. Before coming to Fordham, he served on the faculty of Woodstock College from 1960 to 1974 and that of The Catholic University of America from 1974 to 1988. He has been a visiting professor at colleges and universities in the United States and abroad.

The author of over seven hundred articles on theological topics, Cardinal Dulles has published twenty-two books, including *Models of the Church* (1974), *Models of Revelation* (1983), *The Assurance of Things Hoped For: A Theology of Christian Faith* (1994), *The New World of Faith* (2000), and *Newman* (2002). His book *The Splendor of Faith: The Theological Vision of Pope John Paul II* was revised in 2003 for the twenty-fifth anniversary of the papal election.

Past president of both the Catholic Theological Society of America and the American Theological Society, Cardinal Dulles has served on the International Theological Commission and as a member of the United States Lutheran/Roman Catholic Dialogue. He is presently an advisor to the Committee on Doctrine of the National Conference of Catholic Bishops. In 2001 he was created a cardinal of the Catholic Church by Pope John Paul II, the first American theologian who is not a bishop to be named to the college of cardinals.

MARGARET O'BRIEN STEINFELS

Margaret O'Brien Steinfels was editor of *Commonweal* magazine from 1988 until the end of 2002. Leading one of the most influential journals in United States Catholicism, Margaret Steinfels has become a force in the United States Church and religious media for dialogue, inquiry, critical thought, and the honoring of tradition. She was one of two leading lay Catholics asked to address the United States Conference of Catholic Bishops in Dallas in June 2002 on the issue of sexual abuse.

With a bachelor's degree from Loyola University, Chicago, and a master's degree in American history from New York University, Steinfels, a Chicago native born in 1941, entered the world of books, editing, and journalism. In rapid succession, she published a book on day care in America, *Who's Minding the Children?* and became editor first of the *Hastings Center Report* and then social editor for Basic Books. Other editorial posts followed at *Christianity and Crisis, Church,* and the National Pastoral Life Center.

She has shown an uncommon skill for bringing together a great respect for and knowledge of Catholic intellectual tradition with a contemporary resoluteness that this tradition speak to and be affected by the urgent events of our days, from Kosovo, terrorism, and sexual abuse, to welfare and politics. She is married to Peter Steinfels. They have two grown children and one grandchild.

PETER STEINFELS

After serving as senior religion correspondent of *The New York Times* from 1988 to 1997, Peter Steinfels continues to write its biweekly "Beliefs" column on religion and ethics. He is the author most recently of *A People Adrift: The Crisis of the Roman Catholic Church in America* (Simon and Schuster, 2003).

Peter Steinfels was born in Chicago in 1941, graduated from Loyola University there and earned a PhD in European history at Columbia University. He served as editor of *Commonweal* from 1984 to 1988, in addition to earlier service as editorial assistant, associate editor, longtime columnist, and executive editor. He has also been editor of the *Hastings Center Report* and has taught at the University of Notre Dame.

A visiting professor of history at Georgetown from 1997 to 2001, and at the University of Dayton in religious studies in 2005, he recently codirected a major three-year research project on American Catholics in the Public Square, funded by the Pew Charitable Trust.

Peter Steinfels has written over two thousand articles for scores of journals on topics ranging from international affairs to medical ethics. His 1979 book, *The Neoconservatives,* was a pioneering analysis of a major political current. He has for many years written and spoken influentially on religion in the United States, especially on Catholicism, encompassing such topics as the identity of Catholic universities, liberal democracy and secularization, Catholic-Jewish dialogue, health care, and religion and the media.

MARY DOUGLAS

Born in Italy in 1921, and educated by the Sacred Heart nuns and at Oxford, Mary Douglas worked in the Colonial Office during World War II and returned to Oxford to study anthropology in 1946. In 1951 she married James Douglas, obtained a doctorate in philosophy, and jointed the Anthropology Department of University College London, where she stayed for 27 years.

Her research was heavily influenced by the experience of living among the Lele, a tribe in the then Belgian Congo. For example, their ideas about food, health, cleanliness, and classification of animals led her to work on pollution and taboo, which then led to work on modern patterns of public blaming. She also linked her reflections on the Lele to the disciplines of economics and political science.

Comparison between the Lele preoccupation with sorcery and witchcraft and the absence of ancestor cults as a principle of organization also led to several publications, including *Natural Symbols: Explorations in Cosmology* (1970), and editing *Essays in the Sociology of Perception* (1982), and *Thought Styles* (1996). Her interest in religion (both personal and Durkheim-inspired) led her from the Lele rituals to the Bible. Her current interest is reading the priestly work as a post-structural anthropologist (*In the Wilderness* [1993], *Leviticus as Literature* [1999]). Dr. Douglas's other publications include *Purity and Danger* (1966), *Risk and Culture* (1982), *How Institutions Think* (1986), *Risk and Blame* (1992), and *Missing Persons* (1998).

Dr. Douglas has written and edited several other books and articles, and has lectured extensively throughout the world. She has received several honorary degrees and is a member of many editorial boards.

MARY ANN GLENDON

Mary Ann Glendon is the Learned Hand Professor of Law at Harvard University. In 1994, she was appointed by Pope John Paul II to the Pontifical Academy of Social Science and also serves as a member of the Pontifical Council for the Laity. In 1995, she was named to the Holy See's Central Committee for the Great Jubilee 2000. The *National Law Journal* named her one of the "Fifty Most Influential Women Lawyers in America" in 1998.

She has taught at Boston Law School and has been a visiting professor at the University of Chicago Law School and the Gregorian University of Rome. She received her Bachelor of Arts, Juris Doctor, and Master of Comparative Law degrees from the University of Chicago. Professor Glendon studied at the Université Libre de Bruxelles and was a legal intern with the European Economic Community.

Professor Glendon's publications include *A World Made New: Eleanor Roosevelt and the Universal Declaration of Human Rights* (2001), *Comparative Legal Traditions* (1999), *A Nation Under Lawyers* (1994), *Rights Talk: The Impoverishment of Political Discourse* (1991), *The Transformation of Family Law* (1989), and *Abortion and Divorce in Western Law* (1987).

In addition to these publications, Professor Glendon has authored several articles and has lectured widely in this country and in Europe. She has received honorary doctorates from numerous universities.

MARCIA L. COLISH

Marcia Colish was born in Brooklyn, New York. She is a graduate of Smith College and received her doctoral degree from Yale University.

She has been a visiting scholar at Harvard University and Weston School of Theology. Dr. Colish was a fellow at the Woodrow Wilson Center from 1994 to 1995. She received the Haskins Medal from the Medieval Academy of America in 1998. She taught at Skidmore College (1962–63) and Oberlin College (1963–2001), from which she retired as Frederick B. Artz Professor of History. Since then she has been visiting fellow in history at Yale and has taught as visiting professor of history and religious studies (2003) and as lecturer in history (2004–5).

Dr. Colish's publications include *Ambrose's Patriarchs: Ethics for the Common Man* (2005), *Medieval Foundations of the Western Intellectual Tradition, 400–1400* (1999), *Peter Lombard* (1994, ed.), *The Stoic Tradition from Antiquity of the Early Middle Ages, II: Stoicism in Latin Christian Thought through the Sixth Century* (1990), *The Stoic Tradition from Antiquity to the Early Middle Ages, I: Stoicism in Classical Latin Literature* (1985), and *The Mirror of Language: A Study in the Medieval Theory of Knowledge* (1983). In addition to these publications, Dr. Colish has authored numerous articles in scholarly journals.

JILL KER CONWAY

Jill Ker Conway was born in Hillston, New South Wales. She is a graduate of the University of Sydney in history and english (1958) and received her doctoral degree from Harvard University (1969).

Dr. Conway served as vice president for internal affairs at the University of Toronto from 1973 to 1975. In 1975, she became the first woman president of Smith College. Since 1985, she has been a visiting scholar and professor in the Massachusetts Institute of Technology's Program in Science, Technology, and Society. She is a noted historian, specializing in the experience of women in America, and now lives in Milton, Massachusetts.

Dr. Conway's publications include *When Memory Speaks* (1998), *Written By Herself,* vols. 1 and 2 (1992, 1996), *True North* (1994), *The Politics of Women's Education* (1993), *The Road from Coorain* (1989), *Learning about Women* (1989, ed.), *The First Generation of American Women Graduates* (1987), *The Female Experience in Eighteenth and Nineteenth Century America: A Guide to the History of American Women* (1982), and *Merchants and Merinos* (1960). In addition to these publications, Dr. Conway has authored numerous articles in scholarly journals.

DAVID TRACY

David Tracy is the Andrew Thomas Greeley and Grace McNichols Greeley Distinguished Service Professor of Catholic Studies and professor of theology and the philosophy of religion in the University of Chicago Divinity School. He received an STL (licentiate in theology) in 1964 and STD (doctorate in theology) in 1969 from Gregorian University in Rome. He also serves in the Committee on Social Thought. Professor Tracy teaches a wide variety of courses in contemporary theology, offering classes in philosophical, systematic, and constructive theology and hermeneutics, and courses dealing with issues and persons in religion and modern thought. His publications include *The Analogical Imagination: Christian Theology and the Culture of Pluralism* (1981), *On Naming the Present: Reflections on God, Hermeneutics, and Church* (1995), *Plurality and Ambiguity: Hermeneutics, Religion, and Hope* (1987), and *Blessed Rage for Order* (1975). Professor Tracy is currently writing a book on God.

GUSTAVO GUTIÉRREZ

Gustavo Gutiérrez was born in Lima, Peru, in 1928. After studies in medicine and literature in Peru, he studied psychology and philosophy at Louvain, and eventually took a doctorate at the Institut Catholique in Lyons. He is currently the John Cardinal O'Hara Professor of Theology at the University of Notre Dame.

He is most well known for his foundational work in Latin American liberation theology, *A Theology of Liberation: History, Politics, Salvation* (1973). His other major books touch as well on issues of spirituality and Latin American history, and include *We Drink from Our Own Wells: The Spiritual Journey of a People, On Job: God-Talk and the Suffering of the Innocent, The Truth Shall Make You Free, The God of Life*, and *Las Casas: In Search of the Poor of Jesus Christ*. His essays have appeared in several journals, and he has also published in *Concilium*.

Gutiérrez has been a principal professor at the Pontifical University of Peru, and has been visiting professor at many major universities in North America and Europe. He is a member of the Peruvian Academy of Language, and in 1993 he was awarded the Legion of Honor by the French government for his tireless work for human dignity and life, and against oppression, in Latin America and the third world. He is currently working on a book exploring the historical background and continuing theological relevance of the preferential option for the poor.

CHARLES TAYLOR

Charles Taylor is a Canadian philosopher known for his viewpoints on morality and modern Western identity of individuals and groups. He is one of the leading theorists of the intellectual movement known as communitarianism and is considered to be among the key thinkers laying the foundation for communitarian thought. His principal philosophical standpoint is that of "exclusive humanism"—a humanism without reference to the transcendent, especially as it relates to cultural, social, or political life.

Taylor was educated at McGill University (BA in history in 1952) and at Oxford (BA in politics, philosophy, and economics in 1955, MA in 1960, PhD in 1961). He worked as professor for moral philosophy at Oxford University and as professor for political sciences and philosophy at McGill University in Montreal, Canada, now as professor emeritus. Taylor now has a part-time appointment as a Board of Trustees Professor of Law and Philosophy at Northwestern University in Evanston, Illinois. In 1995 he was made a Companion of the Order of Canada.

Over the decades, Professor Taylor has been involved in Quebec and Canadian politics. He was a candidate for the Federal Parliament on behalf of the New Democratic Party on a number of occasions during the 1960s, and also served on the executive committee of the party until 1976. He has been actively engaged on the federalist side in the two referenda on Quebec independence, in 1980 and 1995.

His noted books include *Hegel* (1975), *Hegel and Modern Society* (1979), *Sources of the Self: The Making of Modern Identity* (1989), and *The Malaise of Modernity* (1991; the published version of Taylor's Massey Lectures, reprinted in the United States as *The Ethics of Authenticity*, 1992).

Index